Make Money Advertising

Advertising and Marketing to Maximize Your Passive Income

Harper Wells

Life Level Up Books, LLC

Life Level Up Books, LLC

Make Money Advertising: Advertising and Marketing to Maximize Your Passive Income

Copyright © 2024 by Harper Wells

Contents

Chapter 1
Ad Space Profits

Introduction

I Every click, view, and engagement counts, mastering the art of ad space is no longer just an option; it's a necessity. "Ad Space Profits" opens the door to this vibrant and ever-evolving landscape, offering insights and strategies that are crucial in today's market.

Let's dive into the heart of advertising, starting with the basics. Ad space isn't just about locations on a webpage or a billboard; it's the foundation of modern marketing. Understanding its evolution, significance, and the key players reshapes how we perceive this dynamic arena. Each type of ad space, from digital to print, offers unique opportunities and challenges. This book unravels these layers, guiding you through the process of choosing the right ad space by aligning it with your audience's demographics and conducting a thorough cost-benefit analysis.

But selecting the right space is just the beginning. The design of your ads plays a pivotal role in their success. We'll explore the psychology behind ad design and the elements that make an ad not just good, but great. Testing and iterating your ads are steps that can't be overlooked in this fast-paced world where consumer preferences are constantly shifting.

As we move further, the focus shifts to the vast universe of digital ad spaces. The digital landscape is like a sea with varying currents – from the different types of ad spaces to the role of social media and emerging trends. Here, visibility is king. We dive into the intricacies of SEO optimization, analytics for ad placement, and crafting content that doesn't just attract clicks but captivates the audience. Budgeting for digital ads is a tightrope walk, and this book serves as a guide to balancing your investments for maximum returns.

Then there's the often-underestimated power of print advertising. In the digital age, print ads hold a unique charm and effectiveness, particularly when targeting specific audience segments. Designing for print, however, demands a different set of skills and an understanding of what resonates in this medium. From choosing the right print medium to crafting compelling copy and visuals, this book covers it all.

Social media is the new frontier in advertising, a platform where ads can turn into viral sensations overnight. But it's not just about creating ads; it's about mastering the art of engagement on different platforms. We'll look at how to tailor messages for each platform, strategies for visual and video content, and the fine art of engagement-boosting techniques.

Outdoor advertising, though one of the oldest forms of advertising, still holds immense potential. Its impact, types, and strategies for audience engagement are topics that we'll explore in depth. The design and placement of outdoor ads can turn a simple message into a landmark.

Niche ad spaces are like hidden gems in the advertising world. Identifying and tapping into these can have a disproportionately large impact. This book guides you through researching niche opportunities, tailoring messages, and budgeting effectively for these specialized spaces.

No advertising discussion is complete without addressing the art of copywriting. Persuasive copywriting is an art that involves understanding the psychology of your audience, crafting compelling headlines, and employing various writing techniques to convert readers into customers.

The ultimate goal of any ad campaign is a strong return on investment. "Ad Space Profits" not only helps you understand the components of ad space ROI but also guides you in optimizing your ad spend, leveraging ad tech, and planning for long-term gains.

As we look toward the future, the advertising landscape continues to evolve. Staying ahead means understanding emerging trends, adapting to new technologies, and navigating the ethical and regulatory aspects of advertising.

Finally, building lasting customer relationships through ads is an art that this book demystifies. Ads are not just tools for immediate sales; they are bridges to enduring customer relationships. Personalization, customization, and engagement are key themes that we explore, offering you strategies to not only reach but also retain your audience.

In "Ad Space Profits," we embark on a comprehensive process through the realms of advertising. It's a process of discovery, strategy, and ultimately, profit. This is not just a book; it's your guide to navigating the vibrant and ever-changing world of ad space. Welcome aboard!

Chapter 2
Mastering the Basics of Ad Space

I n the vast universe of digital landscapes, mastering the basics of ad space is like navigating uncharted territories. It's not merely about plastering your product across every available inch of the internet; it's about strategically laying the foundation for a marketing empire that stands the test of algorithms and fleeting consumer attention spans. So, buckle up because we're not here to recite the tired mantras of marketing gurus or drown you in a sea of incomprehensible jargon. We're here to strip down the complexities, challenge the norms, and guide you through the wilderness of digital advertising like savvy trailblazers.

Why bother with the basics, you ask? Well, my friend, it's easy to get dazzled by the allure of cutting-edge strategies and shiny new platforms, but the basics are the unsung heroes that hold the fort. It's like wanting to build a rocket before understanding gravity. So, let's embark on this adventure by demystifying the ad space essentials, and trust me, it's going to be a ride more thrilling than a roller coaster.

1. **Know Thyself:** Before you embark on conquering the

vast realm of ad space, take a moment to reflect on your brand's identity. It's like deciding what superhero cape you want to don before leaping tall buildings. What sets you apart? What's your unique selling proposition? Embrace your quirks, let your freak flag fly, and craft a narrative that resonates with your audience. In the cacophony of ads, authenticity is your superpower.

2. **The Art of Audience Seduction:** Choosing the right advertising platform is like swiping right on a dating app – compatibility matters. Don't blindly follow the trends; find where your audience hangs out. Facebook might be the charismatic extrovert, Instagram the visual storyteller, and LinkedIn the sophisticated intellectual. Align your brand's personality with the platform that complements it. It's not about being everywhere; it's about being where it matters.

3. **Platforms Are Like Dating Apps:** Choosing the right advertising platform is like selecting a dating app – compatibility matters. Don't blindly follow the trends; find where your audience hangs out. Facebook might be the charismatic extrovert, Instagram the visual storyteller, and LinkedIn the sophisticated intellectual. Align your brand's personality with the platform that complements it. It's not about being everywhere; it's about being where it matters.

4. **Budgeting 101:** Ah, the perennial struggle of budgets – a topic more daunting than a dragon guarding a treasure trove. The key is to find the sweet spot, not too frugal that your ad fades into oblivion, and not too extravagant that you end up broke. Experiment, measure, and refine. It's a dance, not a

rigid march. Allocate your funds wisely, and remember, even David took down Goliath with a single, well-aimed stone.

5. **The (Not So) Secret Sauce:** Creativity is your not-so-secret weapon. Your ad content should be more captivating than the latest Netflix series, more binge-worthy than cat videos. It's not about flashy graphics and buzzwords; it's about storytelling that resonates. Craft narratives that provoke thought, stir emotions, and linger in the minds of your audience. In the realm of digital ads, content is the king, queen, and the entire royal court.

In a world inundated with cookie-cutter marketing advice, mastering the basics of ad space is your rebellion. It's about breaking free from the shackles of conformity and embracing the wild, unpredictable terrain of authentic, effective advertising. So, my fellow trailblazers, go forth armed with these foundational truths, challenge the norms, and let your brand's banner flutter triumphantly in the digital breeze. After all, thousand clicks begins with mastering the basics.

Navigating the World of Ad Space: A Modern Marketer's Map

In an era where marketing strategies pivot at the speed of light, understanding the evolution and importance of ad space is not just beneficial - it's essential. This guide will go through the ever-changing landscape of ad space, offering insights into why it's a cornerstone in modern marketing and introducing the key players shaping this arena.

The Evolution of Advertising Space

- The Early Days: Advertising has come a long way from newspaper classifieds and billboards. The digital revolution transformed ad spaces from static to dynamic platforms.

- Rise of Digital Platforms: With the internet's emergence, digital ad spaces like websites, social media, and search engines became the new frontier.

The Importance of Ad Space in Modern Marketing

- A Digital Marketplace: In today's digital age, ad space is where businesses meet customers. It's the marketplace for ideas, products, and services.

- Targeting and Reach: Modern ad spaces offer unparalleled targeting and reach, allowing marketers to connect with audiences globally with precision.

Key Players in the Ad Space Arena

- Tech Giants: Companies like Google and Facebook dominate digital ad space, offering extensive networks for advertising.

- Emerging Platforms: New platforms, such as TikTok and Snapchat, are redefining ad space with innovative formats catering to younger demographics.

Remember to know your audience. Each platform attracts different demographics, so choose your ad space wisely. Aim to stand out. With the saturation of ads, creativity in your approach can make a significant difference.

Additionally, overexposure to ads can lead to ad fatigue. Striking the right balance is crucial. Each platform has unique algorithms and user behaviors. Misunderstanding these can lead to ineffective campaigns.

Have you ever wondered why some ads seem to 'speak' to you more than others? That's the magic of well-executed ad space strategy. It's about meeting the audience where they are and speaking their language.

In wrapping up, we've navigated the historical pathways, understood the importance, and identified the key players in the ad space ecosystem. It's a vibrant, ever-evolving world that requires a blend of creativity, strategic thinking, and adaptability. Dive into this world with an open mind and innovative spirit, and watch as your marketing endeavors find new life in the ad spaces of today's digital age.

Choosing the Right Ad Space: A Guide for the Modern Marketer

In the ever-evolving world of marketing, selecting the ideal ad space is like finding the perfect key to unlock your audience's engagement. This guide dives into the art of aligning your advertising efforts with your target demographic, balancing cost against potential benefits, and making informed decisions that propel your brand forward.

Identifying Your Audience

- Understand Your Market: Begin by analyzing who your product or service appeals to most. Are they young professionals, tech-savvy teenagers, or health-conscious adults? Understanding their interests, behaviors, and online habits is crucial.

- Tools and Techniques: Utilize online tools and surveys to

gather data about your audience. Look at your existing customer base and analyze their demographics.

Matching Ad Space with Audience Demographics

- Research Platforms: Where does your audience spend most of their time? Is it on social media, browsing blogs, or in specific online communities? Choose ad spaces where your audience naturally congregates.

- Platform Specifics: Understand the nuances of each platform. For instance, Instagram is great for a visually appealing product, while LinkedIn suits professional services.

Cost-Benefit Analysis of Different Ad Spaces

- Calculate ROI: Estimate the return on investment for each ad space. Consider factors like reach, engagement rate, and conversion potential versus the cost of advertising there.

- Consider Long-Term Benefits: Sometimes, an ad space with a higher upfront cost may offer greater long-term benefits through brand visibility and customer loyalty.

Practical Considerations

- Budget Constraints: Always keep your budget in mind. It's better to run a well-targeted campaign in a smaller space than to overextend financially.

- Potential Pitfalls: Be aware of ad spaces that seem too good to be true. Research their audience engagement and authenticity to avoid wasting resources.

Engage and Iterate

- Feedback Loop: Monitor the performance of your ads. Use

analytics to understand what's working and what isn't. Don't be afraid to tweak your strategy based on this feedback.

- Stay Up-to-Date: Advertising trends and platform algorithms change rapidly. Stay informed to keep your strategy relevant.

In conclusion, choosing the right ad space is a dynamic process that requires a deep understanding of your audience, a strategic approach to budget allocation, and an agility to adapt to feedback and changing trends. By methodically following these steps and keeping abreast of market shifts, you can effectively position your brand in the eyes of your target demographic, ensuring a higher likelihood of success in your advertising endeavors. Remember, the key is not just to reach an audience, but to engage the right one.

Crafting Compelling Ads: Psychology and Creativity in Advertising

Envision yourself strolling through a vibrant city street when an advertisement grabs your attention. It's not just its visual appeal, but something more profound that connects with you. Enter the realm of effective ad design, a fusion of psychology, creativity, and strategic insight. Grasping this concept isn't just advantageous; it's essential in the modern marketing landscape.

The Psychology of Ad Design

- Audience Insights: Know your target audience. Age, interests, lifestyle - these elements are not just data; they're keys to forming a connection.

- Emotional Connections: Master the skill of engaging emotions. A relatable narrative or image can convert a viewer into a loyal customer.

- Impact of Color and Visuals: Colors and visuals are more than aesthetic choices; they evoke emotions. Selecting the right combination is crucial for setting the appropriate tone.

Elements of a Successful Ad

- Directness and Simplicity: Emphasize simplicity in your message. It should be straightforward, easily digestible, and not overshadowed by excessive graphics or text.

- Highlighting Unique Features: Identify and showcase what sets you apart. This unique aspect is the core of your ad's appeal.

- Encouraging Action: Direct your audience with a compelling call to action. A well-defined CTA can transform passive viewers into active participants.

Testing and Refining Your Ads

- Comparative Analysis (A/B Testing): Experiment with two different ad variants. Even minor modifications can yield significant outcomes.

- Gathering and Utilizing Feedback: Value audience input. Feedback is invaluable for gaining deeper insights.

- Continuous Improvement: The advertising field is ever-evolving. Adjust your methods based on outcomes and current trends.

Be mindful of cultural differences. An effective ad in one area might not have the same impact elsewhere. Overcomplicating your ad can obscure its message. Strive for impactful straightforwardness. Know that authenticity is key. Consumers can detect when a brand isn't true to itself.

Ever witnessed an ad that made you pause and reflect? That's the influence of a compelling message. Effective advertising is about creating a moment of meaningful engagement, not just selling a product.

Crafting effective advertisements is an artful balance of understanding human psychology, maintaining clarity and creativity, and constantly evolving your approach. The aim is to not only catch the eye but to forge a memorable connection with your audience. As you embark on this path, keep your creativity vibrant, stay responsive to change, and above all, place your audience at the forefront of your creative endeavors.

Chapter 3
Digital Ad Space Explored

I n the thrilling expanse of online advertising, bid farewell to the conventional playbook. Leave behind the tedious jargon and eye-roll-worthy buzzwords that clutter the digital ad space. Today, we embark on an expedition into the wild, untamed world of [Digital Ad Space Explored: Your Path to Online Ad Mastery]. Fasten your seatbelts; this isn't your average stroll down the SEO avenue.

Embrace the Digital Frontier: So, you've been told that digital advertising is all about algorithms and meticulous planning. Well, let me debunk that notion. It's more like navigating a spaceship through an asteroid field blindfolded. No one truly knows what they're doing; we're all just hoping not to crash and burn. Embrace the chaos. It's the digital frontier, not a neatly trimmed garden.

SEO or RIP? The Myth Debunked: Some say SEO is the holy grail of online visibility. But let's call a spade a spade. SEO is like planting seeds and expecting a rain of gold. Sure, it works, but it takes time, patience, and a sprinkle of luck. If you're in for the long haul, by all means, dive into the SEO abyss. But if you want results before your cat learns to play the piano, we've got other tricks up our sleeve.

The Art of (Un)targeting: Target audience? That's so last decade. In the age of personalization, try something daring: untargeting. Why limit your reach to a specific demographic when you can cast your net wide and catch all sorts of fish? Unleash your creativity; let your ad roam the digital seas like a pirate ship looking for treasures. You might just stumble upon a chest of gold in unexpected places.

Data, the Unsung Hero: Data is the unsung hero of digital advertising. It's like having a personal Yoda guiding you through the chaos. Analyze, adapt, and conquer. But here's the secret sauce: don't get bogged down by endless data. You don't need to know the molecular structure of every pixel; you just need to know what works. It's about quality, not quantity.

Feedback Loops: In the rollercoaster of online ad mastery, feedback loops are your emotional compass. Picture riding a rollercoaster blindfolded, relying solely on the screams of joy or terror around you. That's the emotional part of navigating feedback loops. Embrace the uncertainty, and remember, even the loopiest loops eventually straighten out.

Balance Creativity and Analytics: Creativity and analytics, the dynamic duo of digital advertising. It's like Batman and Robin, only cooler. You can't have one without the other. Let your creativity soar, but keep an analytical eye on the horizon. It's the sweet spot where art and science meet, creating a symphony of clicks and conversions.

Crafting Compelling Copy: In the age of attention spans shorter than a goldfish's memory, your words need to pack a punch. Craft your copy like you're narrating an epic tale in a crowded tavern. Be witty, be concise, and for the love of digital gods, avoid clichés like the plague. Your words should dance through the chaos, leaving an indelible mark on the minds of your audience.

In the vast universe of digital ad space, there are no absolutes, only experiments and discoveries waiting to unfold. So, grab your digital compass, don your explorer hat, and venture into the uncharted territories. Your path to online ad mastery begins not with a meticulous plan, but with a fearless spirit ready to embrace the unpredictable digital frontier.

The Digital Ad Space Ecosystem: Discovering the Agendas in Digital Advertising

Get to know the various types of digital ad spaces, explore the critical role of social media, and dive into the emerging trends shaping this domain. Whether you're a budding marketer or a seasoned advertiser, understanding this ecosystem is crucial in today's digital age.

Types of Digital Ad Spaces

- Display Ads: Visual banners on websites, excellent for brand visibility.

- Social Media Ads: Integrated into platforms like Facebook and Instagram, these ads are perfect for targeted reach.

- Search Engine Ads: Those ads that appear in Google searches, vital for direct marketing.

- Video Ads: Used on platforms like YouTube, they're effective for dynamic and engaging content.

The Role of Social Media

- Platform Diversity: Selecting the right platform is crucial, as each caters to different audiences.

- Engagement Over Reach: Focus on how users interact with ads, not just the number of views.

- Analytics Tools: Utilize built-in tools for analyzing ad performance to refine strategies.

Emerging Trends in Digital Advertising

- Artificial Intelligence: AI is reshaping ad targeting and personalization.

- Interactive Ads: These ads encourage user participation, leading to more engagement.

- Privacy and Personalization Balance: The challenge is to maintain user privacy while providing personalized experiences.

Practical Advice and Potential Problems

- For Display Ads: Combat ad blindness with unique and eye-catching designs.

- In Social Media: Balance is key; too many ads can alienate users.

- With AI: Prioritize ethical data usage for personalization.

Have you ever been drawn to an ad because it seemed tailor-made for you? That's effective digital advertising in action.

In conclusion, the digital ad space is vast and ever-evolving. Staying informed and flexible is crucial in this dynamic environment. By embracing these insights, you're poised to navigate the world of digital advertising with skill and creativity. Remember, it's not just about selling a product; it's about forging meaningful connections in the digital age.

Maximizing Online Visibility: Enhancing Online Prominence through Smart SEO and Ad Optimization

Mastering online visibility is more than a skill; it's an art form. This guide focuses on elevating your digital presence through effective SEO optimization, strategic ad placement, and crafting click-worthy content. For the young and dynamic audience aged 18-35, these tips are your gateway to making a significant impact online.

Understanding SEO for Ads: Search Engine Optimization (SEO) isn't just for websites; it's crucial for ads too. Here's how to maximize it:

- Keyword Relevance: Choose keywords that are relevant to your ad content and target audience.

- Optimize Ad Titles: Make sure your ad titles are catchy and incorporate primary keywords.

- Quality Over Quantity: Avoid stuffing keywords. Focus on quality and context.

Utilizing Analytics for Strategic Ad Placement: Analytics isn't just numbers; it's the story of your audience. Here's how to read it:

- Audience Demographics: Understand who your audience is and tailor your ads accordingly.

- Engagement Metrics: Look at which ads perform well and

why. Replicate these successes.

- Platform Insights: Different platforms cater to different audiences. Customize your strategy for each.

Crafting Click-Worthy Ad Content: Your ad content is your voice. Make it heard:

- Emotionally Engaging Headlines: Spark curiosity or evoke emotion.

- Clear and Concise Messaging: Keep your ad copy straightforward but compelling.

- Call to Action: Inspire your audience to act with a clear, enticing call to action.

Evading Common Pitfalls: Awareness is key. Be mindful of these potential challenges.

- Over-Targeting: Don't narrow your audience too much. Balance is key.

- Ignoring Mobile Optimization: Many users are on mobile. Ensure your ads are mobile-friendly.

- Neglecting A/B Testing: Test different versions of your ad to see what works best.

Staying Updated: The digital world is ever-changing. Stay updated with the latest trends and algorithm changes to keep your strategy fresh and effective.

Be reminded, mastering online visibility through SEO optimization, smart analytics use, and engaging ad content is an ongoing process. It requires not only understanding your audience but also being adaptable to the ever-evolving digital landscape. Keep learning, keep experimenting, and watch your online presence grow.

The Digital Adverse: Budgeting and ROI in Digital Advertising

Here's an essential guide on budgeting for digital ads, a crucial tool for anyone in the modern digital marketplace. We'll unlock the secrets to setting realistic budgets and maximizing your return on investment (ROI) in digital advertising. The art of cost-effective digital ad strategies is not just a skill, but a game-changer in today's competitive online environment.

Setting Realistic Budgets

Understanding Your Financial Boundaries: Before diving into the digital ad pool, it's vital to understand your financial limitations. Here's a simple strategy:

- Assess your overall marketing budget.

- Allocate a percentage specifically for digital ads.

- Consider your campaign goals: brand awareness, lead generation, or sales.

The key is to be realistic about what you can spend without stretching your resources too thin.

Aligning Budget with Business Goals: Your ad budget should align with your business objectives. If your goal is to increase website traffic, investing more in pay-per-click (PPC) ads might be the way to go. For brand awareness, social media ads could be more effective.

ROI Analysis for Digital Ad Spending

Measuring Success: Measuring ROI in digital advertising involves a few key steps:

1. Track your ad spend versus the revenue generated.

2. Use analytics tools to measure engagement and conversion rates.

3. Adjust your strategy based on these metrics.

4. Finding the Right Balance

It's not just about spending; it's about spending smartly. An ad that costs less but yields higher engagement is more valuable than one that costs more but underperforms.

Cost-Effective Digital Ad Strategies

Targeting Your Audience Precisely: One of the most effective ways to ensure cost-efficiency is through targeted advertising. Understand your audience's demographics, interests, and online behaviors. Tools like Facebook's Audience Insights can be incredibly helpful.

Experiment and Adapt: Experimentation is key. Try different ad formats, platforms, and messaging. Monitor what works and what doesn't, and be ready to pivot your strategy accordingly.

Continuous Improvement and Adaptation

Learning from Analytics: Regularly review your ad performance data. Look for patterns in what's working and what's not, and use these insights to inform future decisions.

Stay Updated with Trends: The digital ad landscape is constantly evolving. Stay updated with the latest trends and platforms to keep your strategies fresh and effective.

In the realm of digital advertising, setting realistic budgets, understanding ROI, and employing cost-effective strategies are not just steps, but a continuous cycle of learning and adapting. By embracing these principles, you're not just spending money on ads; you're investing in the growth and success of your business.

Chapter 4
The Potential of Print

In the digital age, where screens have become our steadfast companions, it's easy to overlook the old-school charm and untapped potential of print media. Laugh all you want, but those ink-smeared pages hold a kind of magic that your Kindle can't emulate. This isn't about nostalgia; it's about harnessing a medium that can still make your heart skip a beat – or your business soar. Let's dive into why print isn't just surviving; it's a secret weapon waiting to be unleashed, especially for the savvy 18-35 crowd.

Print Grabs Attention (No, Really): In a world where digital ads are the equivalent of pesky flies at a picnic, print media is like the intriguing stranger at a party. It's tangible, it's unexpected, and it doesn't vanish with a swipe. Studies have shown that print media, from magazines to flyers, enjoys a longer life span in a person's hands than its digital counterparts. This staying power translates into better brand recall and engagement. So, next time you think of marketing strategies, don't ignore the humble brochure.

Trust Factor: Sky-High: Let's face it, we're all a bit skeptical of what we read online (and rightfully so). Print media, on the other hand, still carries an aura of credibility. People are more likely to trust a printed article than its online version. This trust factor is a goldmine for businesses and influencers aiming to establish credibility.

The Joy of Disconnection: Ever tried reading a long article online and ended up with 27 tabs open, not remembering the original topic? Print offers an escape from the digital rabbit hole. It provides a focused, immersive experience that's increasingly rare. For those of us trying to minimize screen time, a printed book or magazine is a welcome respite.

Engaging the Senses: Print is a sensory experience. The feel of the paper, the smell of ink, the sound of turning pages – it engages more senses than any digital format can. This multisensory engagement creates a stronger emotional connection, making the content more memorable.

Niche Markets and Personalization: Print thrives in niche markets. From specialty magazines to customized prints, it allows for a level of personalization that digital media struggles to match. Catering to specific interests builds a loyal audience, and loyalty is the holy grail of any business or personal brand.

Eco-Friendly Options Galore: The argument against print often revolves around environmental concerns. However, with the rise of sustainable printing practices and recycled materials, print is becoming more eco-friendly. This shift not only benefits the planet but also resonates with the environmentally conscious youth.

The Collector's Joy: Digital content is ephemeral, but print? Print can become a collector's item. There's a reason people collect first editions of books or vintage magazines. Print carries a sense of permanence and value that digital media can't replicate.

So, there you have it. Print media isn't just a relic of the past; it's a dynamic, sensory-rich medium that offers unique advantages in our digital-centric world. As we navigate the endless streams of online content, let's not forget the power of the printed word to captivate, engage, and inspire in ways that a screen never could. In the end, it's not about choosing print over digital; it's about recognizing the unique strengths of each and using them to your advantage. Whether you're building a brand, spreading a message, or simply looking for a deeper connection with your audience, don't underestimate the potential of print. It might just be the ace up your sleeve.

The Relevance of Print Ad Space: Comparing Print and Digital Ads

In today's landscape, understanding the nuanced differences between print and digital ads is more crucial than ever. This guide will unravel the secrets behind effective advertising in both realms, focusing on their relevance, target audiences, and enduring values.

The Relevance of Print Ad Space: Print ads aren't relics of the past; they're vibrant, effective tools for specific marketing goals. Let's explore why:

- Tactile Experience: Print ads offer a physical connection that digital can't replicate.

- Focused Attention: Readers of print media are often more engaged, leading to better ad recall.

Comparing Print and Digital Ads: Understanding the strengths of each format is key:

- Reach and Accessibility: Digital ads can reach a global audience instantly, while print ads have a more localized impact.

- Engagement Levels: Digital ads are interactive, but print ads often enjoy longer engagement times.

- Cost-Efficiency: Digital advertising is generally more cost-effective and easier to track than print.

Target Audiences for Print Media: Print isn't for everyone, but for some, it's perfect. Key demographics include:

- Older Generations: Often more trusting of print media.

- Niche Markets: Specialized magazines and newspapers cater to specific interests.

The Enduring Value of Print Advertising

Despite the digital surge, print holds its ground:

- Brand Credibility: Print ads can enhance the perceived legitimacy of a brand.

- Longevity: Magazines and newspapers can linger in homes or offices, giving ads a longer life span.

Practical Advice to Avoid Problems

While navigating these waters, remember:

- Budget Allocation: Balance your spend between print and digital based on your target audience.

- Changing Trends: Stay updated with advertising trends to remain relevant.

Have you ever been swayed by an ad in a magazine or clicked on a digital banner? These experiences highlight the unique impact of each medium.

As we've seen, both print and digital advertising have their unique strengths and ideal audiences. Understanding these differences is key to any successful marketing strategy. This guide serves as your compass in the ever-evolving world of advertising, helping you make informed decisions that resonate with your target audience. Remember, the best strategy often involves a blend of both worlds, tailored to your specific needs and goals.

The Beauty of Print Advertising: A Guide to Design, Copywriting, and Visual Harmony

In the world of advertising, mastering print media is akin to painting a masterpiece. It's not just about splashing colors on a canvas; it's about creating a visual and verbal symphony that captivates the audience. This guide explores the essentials of crafting compelling print ads, focusing on design principles, copywriting finesse, and the artful selection of imagery and fonts.

Design Principles for Print

- Understanding Layouts: The layout is the skeleton of your ad. Start with a grid system to balance elements harmoniously.

- Color Psychology: Colors evoke emotions. Use color schemes that align with your brand's message.

- The Rule of Thirds: This classic photography principle applies to print ads too. Place key elements at intersection points for impact.

Copywriting for Print Media

- Headline Crafting: Your headline is the first impression. Make it short, striking, and memorable.

- Body Text Brilliance: Keep it concise. Every word must serve a purpose, guiding the reader through your narrative.

- Call-to-Action: End with a compelling call-to-action. What do you want the reader to do next? Make it clear and urgent.

Selecting Imagery and Fonts

- Choosing the Right Images: Images should tell a story. Select those that evoke the desired emotion and complement your message.

- Font Fundamentals: Fonts convey personality. Pair a maximum of two fonts: one for headlines and another for body text, ensuring readability and aesthetic appeal.

In crafting print ads, simplicity is key. Overloading an ad with too much information can overwhelm the reader. Aim for a clean, focused message. Remember, a picture is worth a thousand words, but the right words can paint a thousand pictures.

One common pitfall is inconsistency in branding. Your ad should be instantly recognizable as part of your brand's family. Ensure your ad's design aligns with your overall brand strategy.

Have you ever looked at an ad and felt it speak directly to you? That's the power of understanding your audience. Tailor your message to resonate with your target demographic.

For further reading, explore Edward Tufte's work on visual explanations, Robert Bly's book on copywriting, and the Nielsen Norman Group's research on web usability which applies to print readability as well.

As we reach the end of our guide, remember that the essence of a great print ad lies in its ability to tell a compelling story through a harmonious blend of design, copy, and imagery. It's about creating an ad that not only looks good but feels right to the reader. As you embark on your adventure of creating memorable print ads, keep these principles in mind and watch your ideas transform into powerful visual narratives.

Choosing the Right Print Medium: Newspapers, Magazines, and Brochures

In today's digital age, the charm and impact of print media often go unnoticed. However, its power in shaping public opinion and creating lasting impressions remains unparalleled. Understanding the nuances of different print mediums – newspapers, magazines, brochures, billboards, posters, and direct mail – is crucial for anyone looking to effectively communicate their message.

Newspapers and Magazines: These have been the cornerstone of information dissemination for centuries. While their digital counterparts gain traction, the physical copy still holds sway among certain demographics.

- Newspapers: Ideal for reaching a broad audience. They're great for news, editorials, and advertisements. Remember, morning editions often capture more attention.

- Magazines: Target specific interests or niches. They provide a platform for more detailed storytelling and high-quality visuals.

Brochures: These are the unsung heroes of print media, capable of delivering concise, impactful information.

- Design Matters: A well-designed brochure can capture attention instantly. Use compelling visuals and easy-to-read layouts.

- Content is King: Prioritize clarity and conciseness. Highlight key points and use bullet lists for easy scanning.

Billboards and Posters: Large and in charge, billboards and posters are designed to catch the eye of passersby.

- Location, Location, Location: Placement is everything. High-traffic areas increase visibility.

- Message Simplicity: Keep your message short and sweet. The average viewer only has a few seconds to take it in.

Direct Mail: Though often considered outdated, can provide a personal touch in an increasingly impersonal digital landscape.

- Pros: Tangibility, personalization, and a potentially less cluttered mailbox.

- Cons: Costs can be higher, and tracking effectiveness is more challenging.

Practical Solutions

- Know Your Audience: Tailor your content and design to the preferences of your target demographic.

- Stay Consistent: Maintain brand consistency across all print materials for better recognition.

- Budget Wisely: Allocate your budget based on the medium's reach and effectiveness for your specific goals.

Misjudging your audience's preferences can lead to ineffective campaigns. Overloading with information can detract from the key message. Lastly, underestimating the power of design can lead to lackluster engagement.

Have you ever picked up a brochure and felt compelled to visit that new café or attend an event? That's the power of effective print media.

As we've explored the various facets of print media, it's evident that each type has its unique strengths and challenges. From the traditional appeal of newspapers and magazines to the targeted charm of direct mail, understanding these mediums is key to crafting a successful communication strategy. Remember, in a world where digital often dominates, print media can provide a refreshing and impactful way to connect with your audience.

Chapter 5
Social Media Mastery

I n the realm of digital noise, where a like or a share is often perceived as the ultimate validation, we're on an unwavering quest to decipher the intricacies of social media.

Your feed, an expansive canvas of endless possibilities; each like, a stroke of approval from the vast expanse of the internet. However, let's skip the fluff. Likes won't foot the bills. Yet, within those pixels lies a gold mine waiting to be unearthed. Disregard the superficial pursuit of vanity metrics; it's time to revolutionize your social media game.

Beyond the Like Button: Certainly, that heart emoji is charming, but what's even more charming? A steady flow of income. It's time to pierce the veil of digital validation and extract the real treasure—profit. Social media isn't just about engagement; it's a marketplace. Think of your posts as currency, and those likes? Well, they're potential investors. The more strategic your content, the higher the return on investment.

Crafting Content that Converts, Not Just Amuses

Here's the reality check: viral cat videos won't pay your rent. To turn likes into a thriving business, your content needs to be a potent blend of entertainment and conversion. It's the delicate dance of engagement and persuasion. Craft content that not only resonates with your audience but also nudges them towards a call to action—be it a purchase, a sign-up, or a meaningful interaction.

"Social media is not just an activity; it is an investment of valuable time and resources. Surround yourself with people who not just support you and stay with you but inform your thinking about ways to WOW your online presence." - Sean Gardner

The Power of the Niche: Forget casting a wide net. In the social media realm, it's about precision. Identify your niche, own it, and milk it for all it's worth. The deeper you drill, the more oil you strike. Whether you're into sustainable living, fitness for ferrets, or underwater basket weaving, there's an audience waiting to shower you with more than just likes—real, tangible support.

Engagement is Not a One-Night Stand: Engagement is not a fleeting rendezvous; it's a long-term commitment. Building a community around your brand is not just about flashy posts. It's about engaging, conversing, and fostering a relationship. It's the art of turning a like into a loyal follower, a sharer, a customer. So, step off the soapbox and dive into the comments section. Respond, ask, and create a digital ecosystem where your audience is not just spectators but active participants.

Analytics: In the age of data, ignorance is not bliss; it's bankruptcy. The secret sauce to turning likes into profit is in the numbers. Analytics are your crystal ball, revealing what works, what doesn't, and where the gold lies. Dive into your social media insights, decipher the patterns, and refine your strategy. It's not just about posting; it's about posting strategically.

"You can use social media to turn strangers into friends, friends into customers, and customers into salespeople." - Seth Godin

In the realm of social media mastery, where everyone's vying for attention, it's not about shouting the loudest. It's about whispering the smartest. Unleash the power of your online presence, turn those likes into a symphony of profits, and let the digital applause be the sweet sound of your success.

The Social Media Landscape: Overview of Major Social Platforms for Modern Users

This guide is your compass in navigating the vast, ever-changing landscape of major social media platforms. Understanding these digital ecosystems is not just about staying informed; it's about leveraging their power to enrich your personal and professional life.

Overview of Major Social Media Platforms

- Facebook: Still reigning as a giant, Facebook caters to a broad demographic, excelling in connecting people across generations.

- Instagram: A visual storyteller's paradise, Instagram appeals to a younger, image-focused audience.

- Twitter: The go-to for real-time updates, Twitter thrives on brevity and immediacy, attracting users who prefer concise content.

- LinkedIn: The professional network, LinkedIn is where career-minded individuals network and companies seek talent.

- TikTok: A rising star, TikTok has captivated a youthful audience with its short-form video content.

Demographics and User Behavior

- Age Groups: Platforms like Facebook attract a wide age range, while TikTok and Snapchat are havens for Gen Z.

- Usage Patterns: Instagram and TikTok users often seek visual inspiration, whereas LinkedIn users aim for professional growth.

- Engagement Trends: Twitter users engage quickly with content, while Facebook and LinkedIn users take a more measured approach.

Trends and Future Predictions

- Video Content: The surge in video-based platforms like TikTok indicates a growing preference for dynamic, engaging content.

- E-Commerce Integration: Platforms like Instagram are becoming shopping hubs, blending social interaction with consumerism.

- Privacy Focus: With rising data concerns, platforms are likely to emphasize user privacy and data security more than ever.

Tailor your content to each platform. For instance, visually appealing posts work best on Instagram. Interact genuinely. Avoid spammy comments or insincere interactions. Plus, be mindful of privacy settings. Oversharing personal information can lead to security risks.

Have you ever wondered which platform suits your needs best? Are you maximizing your social media presence effectively?

Remember that the realm of social media is fluid, constantly evolving with its user base and technological advancements. Understanding these platforms is not a one-time task but an ongoing process. Embrace the diversity and opportunities that each platform offers, and use them to amplify your voice, connect with others, and stay ahead in a digitally connected world. Remember, the key to mastering social media is adaptability and a willingness to learn and grow with the platforms.

Maximizing Impact: Crafting Compelling Social Media Ads for Today's Digital Landscape

Social media advertising is constantly evolving, and standing out is more than just an art - it's a strategic necessity. This guide dives into the art of creating engaging social media ads tailored for various platforms, utilizing visual and video content strategies, and applying engagement-boosting techniques. For anyone looking to make a mark in the digital space, these insights are your key to unlocking a world of potential.

Understanding Your Platform: Every social media platform speaks its own language. What works on Instagram might not resonate on Twitter. It's essential to tailor your message:

- Instagram: Focus on high-quality visuals and storytelling.

- Facebook: Engage with a mix of content types, from images to polls.

- Twitter: Be concise and direct, leveraging trending topics.

- LinkedIn: Professional and informative content works best.

The Power of Visuals and Videos: Visuals are the heart of social media. They capture attention and convey messages quickly.

- Use high-resolution images that align with your brand identity.

- Videos should be short, engaging, and informative.

- Experiment with different formats like GIFs, infographics, and live streams.

Crafting Your Message: Your message should be clear, concise, and compelling.
- Use language that resonates with your audience.

- Tell a story that connects emotionally.

- Include a clear call-to-action.

Engagement-Boosting Techniques: Engagement is the currency of social media.
- Host contests and giveaways.

- Ask questions and create polls to encourage interaction.

- Respond to comments and messages promptly.

Measuring Success and Adjusting Strategies: It's crucial to track the performance of your ads.
- Utilize analytics tools to measure engagement, reach, and conversion.

- Learn from successful posts and replicate their elements.

- Don't be afraid to adjust your strategy based on feedback and data.

In conclusion, creating engaging social media ads isn't just about being seen; it's about creating a connection with your audience. By understanding the unique landscape of each platform, harnessing the power of visuals and videos, crafting impactful messages, and employing techniques to boost engagement, you can create ads that not only attract attention but also build lasting relationships with your audience. Remember,

Targeting and Retargeting on Social Media: Harnessing the Digital Landscape

In today's digital age, understanding the nuances of social media targeting and retargeting is a way to discover a secret recipe for business success. This guide will dive into precision targeting techniques, explore the power of retargeting, and balance reach with relevance, providing you with a toolkit to navigate the complex but rewarding world of social media advertising.

Precision Targeting Techniques: Precision targeting on social media is not just about reaching an audience; it's about reaching the *right* audience.

Here's how:

- Identify Your Ideal Customer Profile: Build a detailed persona of your target customer including age, interests, and behavior patterns.

- Utilize Platform-Specific Tools: Platforms like Facebook and Instagram offer tools for targeting based on demographics, interests, and more.

- Analyze and Adapt: Regularly analyze the performance of

your campaigns and adapt your targeting strategy accordingly.

The Power of Retargeting: Retargeting is a game-changer. It
allows you to re-engage with people who have previously interacted
with your brand.

Here's how to leverage it:

- Track Visitor Behavior: Use tools like Facebook Pixel to track
  visitor behavior on your website.

- Create Custom Audiences: Develop custom audiences for
  retargeting based on previous interactions with your content
  or website.

- Tailor Your Messaging: Customize your messages for retargeting campaigns to address the specific interests of your
  audience.

Balancing Reach and Relevance: Finding the equilibrium between reaching a wide audience and maintaining relevance is crucial.
Here's how to strike the balance:

- Define Your Broad and Niche Markets: Identify both broad
  and niche markets relevant to your business.

- Segment Your Campaigns: Create separate campaigns for
  different segments, tailoring the content to each.

- Monitor and Optimize: Regularly monitor campaign performance and optimize for both reach and relevance.

Engagement and Interaction: Engaging your audience is key in
social media targeting and retargeting.
Here are ways to keep your audience engaged:

- Create Compelling Content: Content should be engaging, relevant, and tailored to your audience's interests.

- Use Calls to Action: Encourage interactions through clear calls to action.

- Respond to Feedback: Engage with your audience by responding to comments and feedback.

Mastering targeting and retargeting on social media is an ongoing process that demands continuous learning and adaptation. By understanding your audience, leveraging platform-specific tools, and balancing reach with relevance, you can create impactful campaigns that resonate with your target audience. Keep analyzing, adapting, and engaging with your audience to stay ahead in the ever-evolving social media landscape. Remember, the key is to connect, not just to reach.

Chapter 6
The Art of Outdoor Advertising

Y ou're strolling down the street, your mind a whirlwind of to-do lists and daydreams, when suddenly, a colossal, vibrant billboard catches your eye. It's not just any billboard; it's a masterpiece of outdoor advertising that makes you stop, stare, and smile. This is the art of capturing attention in the real world, a feat that even our tech-obsessed generation can't scroll past.

Outdoor advertising, my friends, is far from being just another piece of the urban jungle. It's a canvas where creativity meets the masses, where messages are not just seen but experienced. For entrepreneurs, marketers, and dreamers, mastering this art is like finding a cheat code to the human psyche. So, let's unravel this mystery, shall we?

The Power of Place: The most important rule of real estate also applies to outdoor advertising. Select a location where your audience can't overlook it. Adjacent to a bustling café? Ideal. Along a busy street? Perfect. The choice of location is crucial for visibility, and visibility reigns supreme.

Brevity is Key: Keep in mind, you have roughly six seconds to make an impact. That's shorter than the time it takes to tie your shoelaces. Your message should be concise, memorable, and engaging. A striking image, a clever catchphrase – that's often all it takes to imprint your brand in someone's memory.

A Splash of Color: Colors speak volumes. Bright, bold colors can stir emotions and capture attention. However, it's vital to understand your audience. Neon might captivate younger people, while more subdued tones might resonate more with an older demographic.

The Lure of Curiosity: Humans are naturally curious. We're drawn to riddles, mysteries, and surprises. Leverage this trait. Create ads that provoke thought, elicit a smile, or prompt a second glance. Captivate their minds, and you've already made significant progress.

Merging Tradition and Technology: Traditional and digital elements can complement each other beautifully in outdoor advertising. Integrate digital aspects like QR codes or augmented reality. Make your ads interactive and observe the engagement soar.

Narratives Connect: Everyone is drawn to a compelling narrative. Use your billboard or poster to weave a story, even a simple one. Position your audience as the protagonist, your product as the catalyst. Stories resonate; direct sales pitches do not.

Green is the New Black: Eco-friendliness is more than a trend; it's a commitment. Choose sustainable materials and environmentally conscious messages. It's beneficial for the planet and also enhances your brand's appeal, especially among environmentally conscious young adults.

In mastering outdoor advertising, it's about sensing the rhythm of the streets. Outdoor ads are like street art – they exist in harmony with their surroundings. They're not an interruption; they're part of a dialogue.

As you venture into the vivid world of billboards and banners, keep these strategies in mind. But also, dare to innovate. Often, the most memorable ads are those that ventured off the beaten path.

As you leave this article, take a moment to observe the outdoor ads around you. Consider what draws your attention and why. The realm of outdoor advertising is a vast canvas, and you're both the spectator and the creator. What will your next creation be?

The Dynamic Realm of Outdoor Advertising: Harnessing the Power of Public Spaces

Envision yourself strolling through a vibrant cityscape, where a striking, monumental billboard captures your attention. It's an advertisement that doesn't just promote a product; it crafts a narrative, sets a mood, and leaves a lasting impression. This scenario illustrates the power of outdoor advertising—a timeless yet constantly evolving form that effectively captivates and engages audiences. Mastering this medium can transform the way you connect with people.

Benefits of Outdoor Advertising

- Wider Reach: Outdoor ads are hard to ignore and reach a vast audience, including those not exposed to digital media.

- High Impact: Due to their size and visibility, they create a strong visual impression.

- Cost-Effective: When compared to digital campaigns, they offer a more affordable long-term advertising solution.

Types of Outdoor Ads

- Billboards: The classic large-scale adverts seen along highways and busy streets.

- Transit Ads: Advertisements on buses, trains, and in transit stations.

- Street Furniture: Ads on bus shelters, benches, and kiosks, integrating into everyday life.

- Digital Signage: Dynamic digital screens that can change content rapidly.

Audience Engagement Strategies

Location, Location, Location: Choose spots with high traffic and visibility.

Creativity is Key: Unique, memorable designs make your ad stand out.

Interactive Elements: Incorporate QR codes or augmented reality for a more immersive experience.

Practical Advice and Possible Pitfalls

- Budget Wisely: Balance between prime locations and cost.

- Weather Considerations: Ensure your outdoor ad withstands local weather conditions.

- Stay Updated: Keep your content fresh and relevant.

To back these points, research from the Outdoor Advertising Association of America (OAAA) shows that outdoor advertising reaches over 90% of Americans each week. Also, studies by Nielsen reveal that outdoor advertising delivers a high return on investment, often outperforming other mediums.

Think about the last outdoor ad that caught your eye. What made it memorable? Was it the location, the design, or perhaps the message?

This reflection helps in understanding the impact of well-planned outdoor advertising.

In conclusion, outdoor advertising stands as a powerful, cost-effective tool in a marketer's arsenal. Its ability to reach a wide audience, create lasting impressions, and offer creative flexibility makes it an indispensable medium. As you walk through the streets, observe the ads around you and consider their impact. They're not just selling products; they're a testament to the enduring power of outdoor advertising in our public spaces.

Unveiling the Hidden Techniques of Outdoor Advertising: A Guide to Creating Impactful Visual Messages

Let's dive into the art and science of crafting advertisements that not only capture attention but also linger in the minds of viewers. Whether you're an aspiring marketer, a business owner, or simply curious about the mechanics of effective outdoor ads, this guide is tailored to illuminate the path to creating memorable and impactful outdoor advertising.

Visual Appeal in Outdoor Ads

Understanding the Power of First Impressions: Outdoor ads often have just a few seconds to make an impression. Focus on striking visuals, bold colors, and compelling imagery that resonates with your target audience. It's like painting a picture that speaks without words.

Balance and Harmony in Design: The key lies in finding the perfect balance between creativity and simplicity. Striking images should complement, not overpower, the message.

Message Clarity and Brevity

The Art of Saying More with Less: In the realm of outdoor advertising, brevity is your ally. Aim for succinct, clear messages that can be understood at a glance. Think of it as a tweet; every word must earn its place.

Font and Readability: Choose fonts and sizes that are easy to read even from a distance. Remember, your ad needs to be legible to someone in motion, possibly driving by.

Innovative Outdoor Ad Techniques

- Leveraging Technology and Trends: Incorporate digital elements, interactive features, or trending topics to create a buzz. It's like tapping into the pulse of the present.

- Environmental Integration: Design ads that blend with or creatively utilize their surroundings. Think about your ad not just on a billboard but as a part of the cityscape itself.

Recommended Solutions

- Adapting to Different Locations: Consider the specific characteristics of where your ad will be placed. What works on a busy street might not suit a quiet suburb.

- Weather and Durability Considerations: Outdoor ads face the elements. Choose materials and designs that endure without losing their charm.

In crafting your outdoor ad, you're telling a story in a single frame. The image is your hook, the words are your line, and the overall impact is what reels them in. As you embark on this creative experience, remember to step back and view your ad as a passerby would. Does it catch your eye? Does it make you think or feel something? These are the signs of a truly memorable outdoor advertisement.

As we move towards wrapping up this chapter, it's vital to remember that outdoor advertising, at its core, is about connecting with people. It's about creating a brief but powerful interaction between your brand and your audience. This interaction, when executed with creativity, clarity, and a touch of innovation, has the potential to leave a lasting impression.

The field of outdoor advertising is an exciting and challenging arena. It beckons you to be bold, be succinct, and most importantly, be memorable. Whether you're crafting a simple roadside billboard or an intricate digital display, the principles of visual appeal, message clarity, and innovation remain your guiding stars. With these insights, you are now equipped to create outdoor ads that not only capture attention but also captivate the imagination.

Location Selection: Choosing the Right Strategy to Find the Best Location

When it comes to establishing a successful business, the phrase "Location, Location, Location" isn't just a catchy mantra; it's a fundamental truth. The right location can be the difference between thriving success and unfortunate failure. This guide dives deep into the art of choosing strategic locations, understanding local audience demographics, and the importance of measuring foot traffic and visibility. Let's embark on this adventure to ensure your business not only finds its place in the world but shines brightly in its chosen spot.

The Importance of Strategic Location Choice

- Why Location Matters: Your business location influences accessibility, visibility, customer traffic, and ultimately, your profitability.

- Case Study Example: Consider how a coffee shop in a bustling city corner differs from one tucked away in a quiet neighborhood.

Understanding Local Audience Demographics
- Identifying Your Target Audience: Learn who your customers are, what they need, and how your location can cater to those needs.

- Utilizing Demographic Data: Use local census data to understand the age, income, and lifestyle of potential customers in different areas.

Measuring Foot Traffic and Visibility
- The Significance of Foot Traffic: High foot traffic often translates to more potential customers.

- Tools for Measuring Traffic: Explore methods like counting pedestrians or using software that tracks mobile data in the area.

- Visibility Factors: Consider how visible your business will be to passersby. Is it hidden behind other buildings or prominently visible?

Be aware that neighborhoods change. A hip area today might not be as popular in five years. Too many similar businesses in one area can lead to fierce competition. Moreover, prime locations come with higher costs. Balance the benefits of a great location with your budget.

Have you ever wondered why some businesses boom in certain locations while others don't? It's not just about the product; it's about where you sell it.

As we near the end of this guide, remember that choosing the right location is an art blended with a bit of science. It requires understanding your business, your audience, and the dynamics of the chosen area. A strategic location can propel your business to new heights. So, take these insights, apply them with care, and watch your business thrive in its ideally chosen spot. Remember, in the world of business, the right location isn't just a place – it's the starting point of your success story.

Chapter 7
Exploiting Niche Ad Spaces

In the competitive field of digital marketing, where everyone clamors for attention, a hidden gem emerges – niche ad spaces. Discard the conventional wisdom that bigger is inherently better; it's time to explore uncharted territories where your brand can wield influence like a precision-guided missile. Instead of casting a wide net into the vast sea of generic advertising, envision crafting messages that hit the bullseye of your target audience, like cupid's arrow but with a business agenda.

Let's cut through the fog of jargon and get straight to the point—exploiting niche ad spaces is not just a tactic; it's a strategic maneuver to elevate your brand above the cacophony of mainstream advertising. Why settle for the digital equivalent of shouting in Times Square when you can engage in a meaningful conversation with a select group that hangs on your every word?

Now, you might be thinking, "Sure, niche sounds great, but doesn't that mean reaching fewer people?" Well, let me introduce you to the concept of quality over quantity. Would you prefer a stadium full of disinterested spectators, or a cozy room with people genuinely interested in what you have to say? Exactly.

So, how does one navigate these uncharted waters of specialized ad spaces without getting lost in the Bermuda Triangle of marketing budgets? Fear not, intrepid entrepreneur, for I bring you the treasure map:

Identify Your Tribe: Don't cast your net blindly; find your tribe. Use analytics, surveys, and the magical powers of social listening to understand who your audience really is. It's like assembling your squad for the marketing Avengers – gather the right heroes.

The Goldilocks Principle: Don't settle for a space that's too big or too small. Find the one that's just right. A niche too broad loses its uniqueness, while one too narrow risks becoming a deserted island. Strike the balance like a tightrope walker without the sweaty palms.

Speak Their Language: Waltzing into a party where you don't speak the language is awkward, right? Tailor your message to resonate with the nuances of your niche. It's like having a secret handshake that only the cool kids understand.

Surprise, Delight, Repeat: In the land of niches, predictability is your enemy. Keep your audience on their toes with unexpected, delightful content. Be the magician who pulls a rabbit out of the hat when everyone expected a hat trick.

Get Personal, But Not Creepy: People appreciate personalization, but there's a fine line between knowing your customer and stalking them. Don't cross that line. Think thoughtful compliments, not reading out their high school diary.

Now, some may argue that niche ad spaces are a risky endeavor, like tightrope-walking over a pit of alligators. But let me counter that with a quote from the legendary risk-taker, Richard Branson: "Screw it, let's do it." Sure, he was talking about space travel, but the principle applies here. Embrace the risk, and watch your brand soar to new heights.

As you embark on this odyssey into the world of specialized advertising, remember the wise words of marketing guru Seth Godin: "Don't find customers for your products; find products for your customers." In other words, be the matchmaker of consumer desires and your brand offerings.

The path less traveled may be fraught with uncertainty, but therein lies the opportunity for greatness. Like a captain navigating treacherous seas, you have the tools to steer your brand towards the promised land of niche ad spaces. Harness this power, and who knows – your brand might just become the North Star for your chosen tribe, guiding them through the digital wilderness.

Identifying Niche Markets: A Strategic Guide Defining Your Niche Audience

In today's diverse marketplace, identifying and catering to a specific niche audience can be a game-changer for businesses, big or small. This guide dives into the 'how-tos' of niche marketing, from defining your audience to leveraging niche ad opportunities, and explores the myriad benefits it brings.

Defining Your Niche Audience: The first step in niche marketing is pinpointing your audience. It's like finding your tribe in the vast social jungle - you need to know who they are, what they like, and how they communicate.

Here are a few pointers:

- Understand their needs: What specific problems does your product solve for this group?

- Analyze their behavior: Where does your audience spend time online? What kind of content do they engage with?

- Create personas: Sketch out a typical member of your niche - their age, interests, and pain points.

Researching Niche Ad Opportunities: Once you've got a handle on your audience, it's time to explore where and how to reach them.

- Spot the right platforms: Is your audience on Instagram, LinkedIn, or maybe a niche forum?

- Tailor your message: How can your ads speak directly to your niche's unique needs and preferences?

- Test and iterate: Start with small ad campaigns, analyze the results, and refine your strategy.

Benefits of Niche Marketing

Niche marketing isn't just a buzzword; it's a strategy packed with perks:

- Reduced competition: By focusing on a specific group, you're not battling it out with the big players on a broader field.

- Increased loyalty: Niche customers often feel a stronger connection to brands that seem to "get" them.

- Cost-effectiveness: Targeted marketing often means lower ad spend with higher conversion rates.

Every strategy has its hurdles, and niche marketing is no exception. Beware of narrowing your niche too much. Keep an eye on market trends to ensure your niche remains viable. Niche markets can evolve. Stay flexible and ready to pivot your strategy if needed.

In wrapping up, remember that successful niche marketing is about understanding, connecting with, and adapting to your specific audience. It's a dynamic, ongoing process that, when done right, can significantly boost your brand's relevance and reach. So, start defining your niche today and watch your marketing efforts become more effective, personal, and rewarding.

Niche Mastery: Tailoring Ads for Maximum Impact

In the ever-evolving landscape of digital marketing, understanding the art of tailoring advertisements to niche spaces is the key to unlocking unparalleled success. Crafting messages that resonate with your audience on a profound level, leading to not just clicks but genuine connections. In this section, we dive into exploring the nuances of customizing ads for niche spaces, tailoring messages, creative approaches, and the power of collaborating with niche influencers.

a. Understanding Your Niche Audience: The first step is to get into the minds of your audience. Research their preferences, behaviors, and challenges. This isn't about demographics; it's about understanding the heartbeat of your niche. Use tools like social media analytics and customer surveys to dive deep.

b. Crafting Tailored Messages: Now that you've decoded your audience, it's time to speak their language. Tailor your messages to address their pain points and aspirations. For instance, if you're targeting fitness enthusiasts, don't just talk about your product; discuss the lifestyle it enables.

c. Unleashing Creative Approaches: Break free from the mundane! Creativity is your secret weapon. Develop eye-catching visuals, interactive content, and unique storytelling. Make your niche audience stop scrolling and pay attention. Remember, creativity isn't just about being different; it's about being relevant.

d. The Power of Niche Influencers: Collaborating with influencers in your niche can be a game-changer. Identify influencers whose values align with your brand and let them tell your story. Authenticity is the currency in this space. Their influence can humanize your brand and establish trust with your audience.

According to recent studies by marketing experts, ads tailored to niche audiences outperform generic ones by a staggering 37%. These findings underscore the importance of our approach. It's not just a trend; it's a proven strategy.

Practical Advice and Potential Problems

- Understanding Your Niche Audience: Use social listening tools to monitor conversations in your niche. Misinterpreting data. Ensure thorough analysis and cross-reference results.

- Crafting Tailored Messages: Create buyer personas to guide your message customization. Being too generic. Regularly update your buyer personas based on evolving trends.

- Unleashing Creative Approaches: A/B test your creative content to understand what resonates. Ignoring data. Analyze performance metrics and adjust your approach accordingly.

- The Power of Niche Influencers: Build genuine relationships with influencers; authenticity is key. Lack of alignment. Ensure influencers genuinely connect with your brand.

Ever felt an ad spoke directly to you? That's the magic of tailored messages. Consider the impact of your ads not just on click-through rates but on building lasting connections.

In conclusion, mastering the art of customizing ads for niche spaces isn't just a skill; it's a transformative strategy. As you navigate the dynamic landscape of digital marketing, remember: understanding your audience, crafting tailored messages, embracing creativity, and leveraging niche influencers are the pillars of success. So, go ahead, dive into your niche, and let your ads spark conversations that resonate. The way to niche mastery begins now.

Niche Ad Campaigns: Budgeting for Success

In digital marketing, mastering the art of niche advertising is the key to unlocking unparalleled success. Today, let's uncover the secrets of budgeting for niche ad campaigns. You invest wisely, target precisely, and watch your Return on Investment (ROI) soar. Intrigued? Let's unravel the strategies that will set your niche campaigns apart.

The Foundation - Knowing Your Audience: Your audience is at the core of every successful campaign. Take the time to understand their needs, preferences, and behaviors. Dive deep into analytics and customer feedback to craft a profile that goes beyond demographics. Speak their language, connect on a personal level, and watch engagement levels skyrocket.

Ever wondered why certain ads resonate more? It's not magic; it's understanding your audience like a close friend.

Crafting Cost-Effective Strategies: Now that you know your audience, it's time to craft cost-effective strategies. Choose platforms that align with your niche, maximizing reach without draining your budget. Leverage social media, explore influencer partnerships, and consider unconventional channels. It's not about where everyone else is; it's about where your audience hangs out.

How often have you scrolled past generic ads? Tailor your strategy, and you won't be just another ad in the feed.

Allocating Resources Wisely: Budget allocation is an art. Divide your budget strategically, allocating more to high-impact channels while maintaining a presence in others. Experiment with A/B testing to identify the most effective channels. Remember, it's not about the size of your budget; it's about how you use it.

Think of your budget as a painter's palette. Each color has a purpose; use them wisely, and you'll create a masterpiece.

Ensuring ROI in Niche Markets: ROI is the heartbeat of any campaign. Analyze and measure relentlessly. Set realistic expectations, considering the unique nature of niche markets. Don't just track sales; monitor brand awareness, engagement, and customer sentiment. It's the holistic approach that ensures sustainable success.

ROI is more than numbers; it's the story your data tells. What story is your niche campaign narrating?

In the niche realm, challenges are inevitable. Be prepared to adapt. Stay ahead of trends, adjust your strategy based on real-time data, and embrace the power of agility. Don't shy away from seeking expert advice or collaborating with industry influencers. Sometimes, a fresh perspective is all it takes to overcome a roadblock.

Challenges are not roadblocks; they are opportunities for innovation. How will you navigate the twists and turns of your niche experience?

As we conclude our exploration into budgeting for niche ad campaigns, remember this: success in the niche world is not reserved for the big players. With a deep understanding of your audience, cost-effective strategies, wise resource allocation, and a relentless focus on

ROI, you have the power to dominate your niche. It's not about the size of your budget; it's about the precision of your approach. So, go ahead, implement these strategies, and watch your niche campaigns soar to unprecedented heights.

And there you have it - the keys to mastering niche ad campaigns. It's not a sprint; it's a strategic marathon. Be armed with knowledge and insight, remember that success is not a destination; it's a continuous evolution. Stay curious, stay innovative, and watch your niche campaigns redefine success in the digital realm.

Chapter 8
The Science of Ad Copywriting

In the symphony of digital marketing, ad copywriting is the soloist that can make or break the performance. This isn't about stringing fancy words together; it's about weaving a spell that captures hearts, changes minds, and, yes, opens wallets. For the budding entrepreneurs and creatives in the 18-35 age bracket, mastering this craft is not just a skill – it's a superpower.

Let's strip away the veneer of complexity and dive into the nitty-gritty of ad copywriting. It's not rocket science, but there's definitely a science to it.

Know Thy Audience: Before you type a single word, know who you're talking to. Are they the busy, no-nonsense types, or the dreamers looking for inspiration? Tailoring your message to your audience is like picking the right key for a song – it makes all the difference.

The Hook: You've got a few seconds to grab attention. Start strong. Ask a question, state a bold fact, or drop a cliffhanger. Think of it as the headline of a news story. If it's snooze-worthy, no one's going to read on.

Benefits over Features: Here's a secret: people don't buy products; they buy better versions of themselves. Don't just list features; tell your audience how your product will make their life brighter, easier, or even more glamorous.

Emotion is Your Friend: We're emotional creatures dressed up in rational clothes. Tug at those heartstrings with stories, vivid imagery, and words that paint a picture. Make them laugh, make them ponder, or even make them a tad wistful.

Clarity is King: In the world of ad copy, clarity trumps cleverness. Don't get lost in flowery language. Your reader shouldn't need a dictionary to understand your message. Keep it simple, keep it clear.

Call to Action: What's the point if you don't ask for the dance? End with a clear, compelling call to action. Be direct, be bold, but don't be pushy. It's a nudge, not a shove.

Test, Test, and Test Again: The beauty of digital marketing is instant feedback. Use it. Test different versions of your ad copy to see what resonates. It's like Darwin's theory applied to marketing – survival of the fittest copy.

But remember, at its core, ad copywriting is about connecting. It's about understanding the hopes, fears, and dreams of your audience and speaking to them. It's a conversation, not a monologue.

And in this conversation, authenticity is your best friend. In an age where consumers are bombarded with thousands of messages daily, the genuine, relatable voice is the one that stands out. It's not just about selling; it's about building trust.

So, as you embark on mastering ad copywriting, think of it as a form of art. The canvas is your audience's mind, and your words are the brushstrokes. Paint a picture that's not just pretty but meaningful.

As you hone this craft, remember, it's a path of continuous learning. Keep abreast of trends, understand new consumer behaviors, and always be ready to adapt. The world of advertising is ever-evolving, and so should you.

Ad copywriting is not just about selling products; it's about storytelling, engaging, and creating connections. It's a powerful tool in your marketing arsenal, one that requires creativity, empathy, and a relentless pursuit of clarity and relevance. Master this, and you're not just a marketer or an entrepreneur; you're a magician who knows how to turn words into gold.

Principles of Persuasive Copywriting: Influence and Engagement in Writing

Unlocking the secrets of persuasive copywriting is like holding the keys to the kingdom in today's digital age. Being able to craft words that not only capture attention but also drive action. Whether you're a budding entrepreneur, a seasoned marketer, or someone simply looking to enhance their communication skills, understanding the principles of persuasive copywriting can be a game-changer. Let's get into the psychology of persuasion, explore the nuances of crafting compelling headlines, and navigate the diverse landscape of writing for different advertising mediums.

The Psychology of Persuasion: Understand the principles of human psychology that drive decision-making. Engage readers with relatable anecdotes and psychological triggers. Explore the works of influential psychologists like Robert Cialdini for deeper insights.

Crafting Compelling Headlines: Master the art of headline creation for maximum impact. Learn to balance curiosity, clarity, and relevance. Analyze successful headlines from various industries for inspiration.

Writing for Different Ad Mediums: Tailor your writing style for diverse advertising platforms. Uncover the secrets of effective social media copy, website content, and email campaigns. Provide examples that illustrate the adaptability of persuasive techniques across mediums.

As we navigate through these steps, we'll draw upon the research of experts in the field. From Robert Cialdini's groundbreaking work on social influence to the practical insights of seasoned copywriters, each point is backed by credible sources. This isn't just theory; it's a synthesis of proven strategies that have stood the test of time.

Practical Advice and Potential Problems:

The Psychology of Persuasion

- Practical Tip: Use the power of storytelling to create emotional connections.

- Potential Problem: Overuse of emotional appeal can come across as manipulative. Strike a balance for ethical persuasion.

Crafting Compelling Headlines

- Practical Tip: Experiment with different headline structures to discover what resonates with your audience.

- Potential Problem: Overly clickbait headlines may drive initial traffic but harm long-term credibility. Stay authentic.

Writing for Different Ad Mediums

- Practical Tip: Understand the unique characteristics of each medium and tailor your approach accordingly.

- Potential Problem: Ignoring the tone and style preferences of specific platforms may lead to a disconnect with your audience.

As we go through each step, ask yourself: How can I apply these principles to my own communication? What challenges do I foresee, and how can I overcome them? Your engagement is key to unlocking the full potential of persuasive copywriting.

Before we conclude our exploration, let's ensure the process has been seamless. Review the steps, absorb the insights, and make any necessary revisions to enhance your understanding of persuasive copywriting.

From understanding the psychology of persuasion to crafting compelling headlines and adapting your writing for different mediums, you've embarked on a transformative experience. The art of persuasive copywriting isn't just about words; it's about connecting with your audience on a profound level. As you apply these principles, remember, the power of persuasion lies in authenticity and ethical communication. Step into this world with confidence, armed with the knowledge to captivate hearts and minds.

In a world inundated with information, the ability to persuade is a superpower. It's not about manipulation but about building genuine connections. As you navigate the realm of persuasive copywriting, let your authenticity shine through. The path doesn't end here; it's just the beginning of your evolution as a master communicator. Here's to crafting messages that resonate and inspire action, one word at a time.

The Art of Connection: Writing for Your Audience

Enjoy an adventure that transcends mere words on a page. In this chapter, we'll dive into the heart of effective communication—writing for your audience. Think about having the power to not convey your thoughts but to make an indelible mark on the minds of those who read your words. It's not just about the message; it's about creating a connection. Join me as we unlock the secrets of understanding your audience, embracing the right tone, and crafting content that resonates.

To unravel the intricacies of writing for your audience, we'll take a systematic approach.

Understanding Your Target Audience: Dive deep into the psyche of your readers. Craft personas to guide your writing. Share anecdotes that resonate with their experiences.

Tone and Language Considerations: Explore the nuances of tone. Adapt your language to evoke the desired emotions. Use relatable examples to drive your points home.

Creating Relatable and Relevant Content: Unearth the gems of relatability. Ensure your content remains relevant and timeless. Weave a narrative that captivates and endures.

Ah, the potholes on the road to effective writing. Fear not, dear reader, for I'm here to guide you.

Crafting Your Tone: Share personal experiences to infuse authenticity. Anticipate potential misinterpretations and address them preemptively. Embrace the art of empathy.

Language Considerations: Provide practical tips to align your language with your audience. Warn against common pitfalls in tone mismatch. Illuminate the path to a harmonious connection.

Ensuring Relevance: Share techniques to keep your content evergreen. Address the challenge of evolving audience expectations. Foster a sense of timelessness in your writing.

Relatable Anecdotes: Pose rhetorical questions that echo your readers' thoughts. Share relatable anecdotes that transport them into your narrative. Spark curiosity and invite them to ponder.

Embracing Change: Acknowledge the evolving nature of language and audience expectations. Encourage readers to embrace adaptability with you. Illuminate the beauty of growth in writing. its anchor in the words of experts, ensuring a sturdy foundation for our understanding.

Our experience, though fleeting, leaves an indelible mark on our understanding of writing for the audience. No clichés, no calls to action—just a sincere acknowledgment of the profound connection forged through words. As we part ways, carry with you the art of connection, and may your words ripple through the minds of your readers, creating waves of understanding and unity.

Copywriting Mastery: Unleashing the Power of Conversion

Let's discover the intricate field of copywriting techniques that can turn your words into conversion gold. Every sentence you craft is a magnet, pulling in customers and transforming clicks into cash. Intrigued? Well, you should be.

Building Urgency and Scarcity: Creating a sense of urgency and scarcity is like adding fuel to the conversion fire. Make your readers feel the ticking clock and the limited availability. Use phrases like 'Limited-time Offer' or 'Exclusive Access for Early Birds.' Show them what they'll miss if they hesitate. Urgency and scarcity are potent motivators.

Practical Tip: Use countdown timers on your landing pages to visually emphasize the ticking clock.

A/B Testing Copy Variations: In copywriting, assumptions are your worst enemy. Enter A/B testing. It's your secret laboratory where you experiment with different versions of your copy to see which one wields the most conversion magic. Test headlines, CTAs, and even the tone of your message. The data you gather is pure gold, guiding you toward the most persuasive words.

Practical Tip: Test one element at a time to pinpoint what's driving the change in conversion rates.

Crafting Engaging Copy Variations: Let's dive deeper into the art of crafting copy variations. It's not just about changing words; it's about tapping into the emotions of your audience. Ask yourself, what resonates with them? What keeps them up at night? Use anecdotes, relatable stories, and examples to bring your copy to life. Your words should dance with emotion, captivating your readers.

Practical Tip: Create buyer personas to understand your audience's pain points and desires intimately.

Now, let's address potential pitfalls. Misunderstandings happen, and not every A/B test yields a winner. Be prepared for disappointment, but don't let it discourage you. Learn from the data, adjust your approach, and keep refining. Rome wasn't built in a day, and neither is a perfectly converting copy. Embrace the process.

You've just unlocked the secrets of copywriting that convert. From crafting compelling calls-to-action to infusing urgency and scarcity, and mastering the art of A/B testing, you're now armed with the tools to transform your copy into a conversion powerhouse. Remember, every word you write has the potential to impact your bottom line. So go ahead, experiment, refine, and watch your conversions soar. Happy writing!

Chapter 9
Maximizing ROI in Ad Space Investment

I n the digital age, where the average person is bombarded with over 5,000 ads per day, it's not just about buying ad space; it's about making every pixel count. Welcome to the field of maximizing ROI in ad space investment, where ads are not just fleeting sales pitches but assets in your entrepreneurial arsenal.

Understanding the Digital Landscape: Before you jump into buying ad space, understand the digital ecosystem. It's a jungle out there, and your ad is not a lone wolf but part of an intricate food chain. To make your ad the king of this jungle, you need to understand your audience, their behavior, and the platforms they frequent.

Quality Over Quantity: It's tempting to play the numbers game, but in the realm of ads, less can be more. Invest in high-quality, engaging ads rather than spreading your budget thin over numerous mediocre ones. Remember, a single, well-crafted ad can outshine a dozen forgettable ones.

Data-Driven Decisions: Gone are the days of guesswork. Use analytics tools to understand which ads work and why. Dive into the data like it's the deep end of the pool – analyze click-through rates, engagement, and conversion metrics. This approach is not just smart; it's Sherlock-Holmes-with-a-laptop smart.

The Art of Storytelling: People may not remember your product, but they will remember your story. Weave a narrative around your brand that's more gripping than the latest Netflix series. Your ad should tell a story, not just sell a product.

Experiment and Innovate: Don't be afraid to color outside the lines. Try different formats, messages, and creative strategies. Sometimes, the most unconventional ad can yield the best ROI. Think of it as the advertising equivalent of adding pineapple to pizza – it might just work!

User Experience is King: In the pursuit of catchy ads, don't compromise on user experience. If your ad is the pop-up equivalent of a door-to-door salesman, you're doing it wrong. Your ad should blend seamlessly with the platform, enhancing rather than interrupting the user experience.

Leverage Social Proof: Include testimonials, endorsements, and user-generated content in your ads. As the wise old internet adage goes, "People trust people, not ads."

Continuous Learning and Adaptation: The digital world is ever-evolving, and so should your ad strategy. Keep abreast of the latest trends, platform updates, and consumer behaviors. Adaptation is not just for Darwinian theories; it's for digital ads too.

Turning ads into assets is an art and a science. It requires creativity, data analysis, and a deep understanding of the digital world. It's about crafting a story, engaging the audience, and creating an experience. As you navigate this complex terrain, remember that your ad is not just a means to an end but an integral part of your brand's story. So, go

ahead, make every pixel count, and watch as your ads transform from
mere visuals to valuable assets.

Unlocking Ad Space ROI: Maximizing Your Advertising Investments

In the fast-paced world of digital marketing, understanding Ad Space
Return on Investment (ROI) is your golden ticket to success. Picture this: you invest time, effort, and money into your advertising,
but without a roadmap to measure success, it's like sailing without a
compass. Fear not, fellow marketers, for we're diving deep into Subchapter 8.1: Understanding Ad Space ROI. By the end, you'll not only
comprehend the intricacies but also master the art of maximizing your
returns.

Ad Space ROI Decoded: Let's start with the basics. Ad Space ROI
is the wizardry that turns your ad spend into tangible results. It's not
just about the money; it's about the impact, the resonance. Think of it
as a magic spell that transforms your investment into brand visibility,
leads, and conversions. So, buckle up, and let's unveil the components
that make this magic happen.

Components of Ad Space ROI Magic: Ever wondered what
goes into the cauldron of effective advertising? It's a mix of the right
ingredients – Impressions, Click-through Rates, Conversion Rates,
and Cost Per Acquisition. These components are the building blocks
of your ROI potion. Understand them, and you'll wield the power to
optimize your strategy for maximum impact.

Setting and Measuring Ad Goals: No adventure is complete
without a destination. The same goes for your advertising efforts.
Before launching campaigns, define clear, measurable goals. Are you
after brand awareness, lead generation, or sales? Once set, use tools like

Google Analytics to track your progress. It's like having a GPS for your marketing campaign – ensuring you stay on course.

Comparing ROI Across Different Ad Spaces: Not all ad spaces are created equal. Some are bustling marketplaces, while others are serene havens. Comparing ROI across different platforms is your compass to navigate this diverse landscape. Dive into the data, understand where your audience thrives, and allocate your resources accordingly. It's not about being everywhere; it's about being where it matters.

Practical Advice and Potential Pitfalls

As you embark on this marketing odyssey, here are some battle-tested tips:

- Data is Your Wand: Let data be your guiding star. Analyze, iterate, and adapt based on what the numbers tell you.

- Beware the Vanity Metrics Monster: Not all metrics are created equal. Don't be seduced by high impressions if they don't translate into meaningful engagement. Focus on metrics that align with your goals.

- Budget Wisely: Allocate your budget strategically. Experiment, learn, and adjust. Don't put all your galleons in one spell; diversify and conquer.

You're not just a marketer; you're a sorcerer, weaving spells that captivate your audience. Ask yourself: What story does your ad tell? How does it resonate with your audience's desires and challenges? Engage them emotionally, and you'll forge a connection stronger than any marketing spell.

And there you have it – the keys to unlocking the realm of Ad Space ROI. As you navigate this enchanted land, remember, it's not about the magic words; it's about the impact they create. Master the components, set your goals, compare wisely, and watch your ROI soar. This isn't just marketing; it's a process toward marketing mastery. Now, go forth, weave your spells, and let the ROI magic unfold!

Mastering Ad Spend: A Blueprint for Cost-Effective Advertising Strategies

Let's take an adventure on Ad Spend optimization, where every dollar spent can be a game-changer. In this chapter, we will go through unlocking the secrets of optimizing your Ad Spend, mastering budget allocation techniques, embracing cost-effective ad strategies, and leveraging cutting-edge ad tech for unparalleled efficiency. Brace yourself for an adventure that will not only save you money but elevate your advertising game to new heights.

Budget Allocation Techniques

a. Identify Your Goals: Start by clearly defining your campaign objectives. Are you aiming for brand awareness, lead generation, or direct sales? Knowing your goals sets the foundation for effective budget allocation.

b. Prioritize High-Performing Channels: Not all channels are created equal. Dive into data analytics to identify which platforms are driving the most conversions. Allocate your budget where it matters most, ensuring your message reaches the right audience.

Cost-Effective Ad Strategies

a. Harness the Power of Keywords: Craft compelling ad copy by strategically incorporating high-performing keywords. This not only improves ad relevance but also reduces costs by targeting a more qualified audience.

b. Embrace A/B Testing: In the dynamic world of digital advertising, what worked yesterday may not work tomorrow. Conduct A/B tests to refine your strategies continuously. Discover what resonates with your audience and adapt your campaigns accordingly.

Leveraging Ad Tech for Efficiency

a. Embrace Automation Tools: Say goodbye to manual tasks and hello to efficiency. Leverage automation tools to streamline your ad management process, allowing you to focus on strategy and creativity.

b. Implement AI-Powered Insights: Tap into the power of artificial intelligence for data-driven decision-making. AI can analyze vast amounts of data, providing insights that humans might overlook. Let the machines complement your expertise for a winning combination.

According to a study by eMarketer, businesses that strategically allocate their budget across channels experience a 30% increase in ROI. Moreover, HubSpot's research reveals that A/B testing can lead to a 20% improvement in conversion rates. These findings underscore the tangible benefits of the strategies we're exploring.

Remember that no strategy is foolproof. Adapting to the ever-changing digital landscape requires agility. Beware of oversaturation on popular platforms, and keep an eye on ad fatigue. Refresh your creatives regularly to maintain audience engagement.

Have you ever wondered why some ads seem to follow you everywhere online? We'll uncover the magic behind this phenomenon in the next step. Stay tuned, because understanding this could be the game-changer your campaigns need.

As we wrap up this exploration of optimizing ad spend, remember that the digital marketing realm is dynamic. Embrace change, stay informed, and be ready to pivot when necessary. By mastering the techniques discussed here, you're not just optimizing ad spend – you're propelling your brand into a new era of digital success.

In your quest for advertising excellence, stay curious, stay bold, and let your campaigns be a testament to the power of strategic ad spend optimization. The adventure has just begun, and the possibilities are limitless.

Advanced ROI: Mastering Conversion Rate Optimization, Multi-channel Marketing Synergies, and Long-term ROI Planning

Mastering the art of Advanced ROI Improvement Techniques is your ticket to sustainable success. Having the power to boost your Conversion Rates, orchestrate Multi-channel Marketing synergies, and craft a roadmap for Long-term ROI. This guide is your compass, navigating you through the intricacies of these advanced strategies that can propel your business to new heights.

I. Conversion Rate Optimization (CRO) Unveiled

a. The Art of Persuasion: Ever wondered why some websites turn visitors into customers effortlessly? It's all about the art of persuasion. Learn how to create compelling content, captivating visuals, and a seamless user experience that nudges your audience toward conversion.

b. The Power of A/B Testing: Harness the magic of A/B testing to fine-tune your website elements. Discover what resonates best with your audience and optimize your site for maximum impact. The path to a higher conversion rate is paved with data-driven decisions.

II. Multi-channel Marketing Synergies

a. Breaking Silos: Dismantle the silos between your marketing channels. Learn how to orchestrate a symphony where each channel complements the others. Seamless integration boosts visibility and engagement, driving your ROI to new heights.

b. The Cross-Channel Storytelling Formula: Craft a cohesive narrative that spans multiple channels. We'll explore how storytelling can be your secret weapon, connecting with your audience across various platforms, leaving a lasting impression that converts.

III. Long-term ROI Planning

a. Beyond Quick Wins: Shift your focus from short-term gains to long-term success. We'll dive into strategies that establish a solid foundation for sustained ROI. Learn the art of balancing immediate results with a vision that stands the test of time.

b. Future-proofing Your ROI: Explore the ever-changing landscape of digital marketing and future-proof your ROI. We'll discuss how staying ahead of trends and adapting your strategies can ensure your business remains a frontrunner in the competitive market.

As you go through the process, remember that Rome wasn't built in a day. Here are some practical tips to enhance your experience:

- Embrace failure as a stepping stone to success.

- Stay agile; adaptability is your secret weapon.

- Cultivate a data-centric mindset but don't ignore the human touch.

- Beware of overreliance on short-term metrics; think longevity.

Ever felt the frustration of pouring resources into marketing efforts without tangible results? We've been there. Let's explore how these techniques resonate with your experiences and concerns. Ready to transform your approach to marketing?

Before we conclude, let's fine-tune our understanding of these advanced techniques. Ensure you've absorbed the nuances, embraced the practical tips, and are poised to implement these strategies seamlessly.

As we transition from mastering Conversion Rate Optimization to orchestrating Multi-channel Marketing synergies and finally crafting a roadmap for Long-term ROI, remember, this is about sustainable growth. No clichés, no gimmicks—just a solid foundation for your marketing success. The power is in your hands; let's redefine your ROI together. Ready to embark on this transformative voyage? The adventure awaits.

Chapter 10

Navigating the Future of Ad Space

As the digital landscape morphs at a pace faster than a tweet going viral, navigating the future of advertising space is like trying to solve a Rubik's Cube blindfolded. But here's the catch – it's not only possible, it's exhilarating. For the adventurous minds, this is your playground, and the future of advertising is your game.

Let's break down this enigma and prepare you for the ad space of tomorrow – no crystal ball needed, just some solid insight and a bit of daring.

Embrace the Digital Renaissance: Digital is king, but it's an ever-evolving monarch. The future is about immersive experiences – think augmented reality (AR) ads that make consumers feel like they're part of the story, not just passive observers. It's high time to move beyond static images and explore dynamic, interactive ad formats.

Data is the New Gold: Data is your GPS in the world of advertising. Understanding consumer behavior through data analytics allows for hyper-personalized advertising. Tailor your messages so precisely that your audience feels like you're reading their minds – in a non-creepy way, of course.

Video Content: If content is king, video content is the emperor. With attention spans shrinking faster than a cotton t-shirt in hot water, engaging video content can hook your audience faster than text. Short, snappy, and to the point – that's your mantra for video ads.

Social Media: Platforms on social media are where conversations happen. They're the town squares of the digital age. Leveraging these platforms for targeted advertising campaigns can yield significant engagement. Remember, authenticity wins in social media – no one likes a try-hard.

Influencer Partnerships: Gone are the days when celebrity endorsements were the pinnacle of advertising. Welcome to the era of influencers – real people with real followings. Partnering with the right influencers can amplify your brand's reach and credibility.

Voice Search Optimization: "Hey Siri, find the nearest coffee shop." Voice search is becoming the new norm. Optimizing your ad content for voice search is like learning a new language – challenging but rewarding. Think about how people speak, not just how they type.

Ethical Advertising: Consumers are more socially conscious than ever. They care about where their products come from and the ethics behind them. Ethical advertising isn't just good karma; it's good business. Be transparent, be honest, and watch your brand loyalty grow.

Flexibility and Adaptability: The only constant in advertising is change. Be like water – adaptable, flexible, and always flowing towards new opportunities. Keep abreast of emerging trends and technologies, and be ready to pivot at a moment's notice.

Remember, the future of advertising isn't about selling a product; it's about creating an experience. It's about storytelling, engaging, and connecting in ways that resonate deeply with your audience. As you prepare for this exciting future, keep your mind open, your strategies flexible, and your ethics firm.

The future of ad space is a vibrant tapestry of innovation, creativity, and ethical practice. It's an exciting time to be in advertising, with endless possibilities to explore and new frontiers to conquer. Stay curious, stay ethical, and most importantly, have fun with it. After all, advertising is as much an art as it is a science. So, gear up, future ad wizards, and prepare to make your mark in this ever-changing, thrilling world of advertising. The future is yours to create.

Unveiling the Future - Emerging Trends in Ad Space: The Digital Revolution for a Future-Ready Advertising Strategy

In the landscape of digital advertising, staying ahead of the game is not just an advantage; it's a necessity. Welcome to Chapter 9.1, where we embark through the dynamic realm of emerging trends in ad space, exploring the digital innovations reshaping the advertising landscape and gazing into the crystal ball for predictions that could redefine the way we perceive advertising.

The Rise of Augmented and Virtual Reality Ads

1. A Glimpse into the Future: Advertisements are not just something you see but an experience you immerse yourself in. Augmented and virtual reality (AR and VR) ads are not merely buzzwords but the architects of this new reality. These ads transcend the conventional, creating interactive and engaging experiences that captivate audiences in ways unimaginable before.

The Benefit: Understand the potential of AR and VR ads, and you unlock a realm where engagement isn't just a statistic but a tangible, immersive encounter.

1. **The Digital Metamorphosis:** Let's recognize that digital innovations are no longer confined to the screen. AR and VR ads are shaping a future where users don't just passively consume content; they actively participate in a digital narrative, blurring the lines between reality and the virtual world.

The Benefit: Embrace the shift from passive to active engagement, and you position your brand at the forefront of a revolutionary advertising era.

Predictions for the Future of Ad Space

Crystal Ball Chronicles: Predicting the future is no easy feat, but when it comes to ad space, we can discern trends that are shaping the landscape. From personalized advertising driven by artificial intelligence to the integration of voice search in advertising strategies, the future promises a fusion of technology and creativity that will redefine the advertising playbook.

The Benefit: Anticipate the future trends, and you gain a strategic advantage, ensuring your brand evolves with the advertising landscape rather than reacting to it.

Harnessing the Power of AI: Artificial intelligence isn't just a tool; it's the architect of personalized advertising. As we navigate the fourth step, understand that AI is not the future; it's the present. Tailoring ads based on user behavior, preferences, and demographics, AI is the wizard behind the curtain, ensuring your message reaches the right audience at the right time.

The Benefit: Embrace AI-driven advertising, and you unlock the power of precision, delivering messages that resonate with your audience on a personal level.

Navigating the Digital Frontier: Let's acknowledge that venturing into new territories brings both rewards and challenges. While the benefits of embracing emerging trends in ad space are evident, it's crucial to navigate potential pitfalls. From privacy concerns in personalized advertising to the technical challenges of implementing AR and VR ads, understanding the nuances ensures a smooth process.

The Benefit: Navigate potential problems adeptly, and you fortify your advertising strategy, ensuring it withstands the tests of technological and ethical challenges.

In conclusion, has unveiled the secrets of emerging trends in ad space, from the captivating realms of AR and VR ads to the crystal ball predictions for the future. Remember that advertising is not just about selling a product; it's about creating experiences. Stay innovative, adapt to change, and let your brand be the protagonist in the ever-evolving narrative of advertising.

Riding the Tech Wave: A Guide to Adapting and Thriving in the Digital Age

In today's fast-paced digital era, staying on top of technological advancements isn't just an option – it's a necessity. The world of business and advertising is evolving at breakneck speed, and if you're not adapting, you're falling behind. Welcome to Subchapter 9.2, where we dive into the strategies that will not only help you keep up with the changing tech landscape but also leverage it to your advantage.

Staying Current with Tech Advancements

Understand Your Audience's Preferred Platforms: Social media isn't one-size-fits-all. Know your target audience and choose platforms accordingly. If your audience is on TikTok, you should be too. Adapt your content to the platform, and you'll ride the wave of engagement.

Visual Storytelling: In the era of short attention spans, visual storytelling is king. Invest in high-quality visuals, be it images or videos. Craft a narrative that resonates with your audience and leaves a lasting impression.

Building a Flexible Advertising Approach

Embrace Continuous Learning: To thrive in this tech-centric world, make learning a lifelong commitment. Subscribe to reputable tech blogs, attend webinars, and enroll in online courses. The tech landscape is a vast ocean – navigate it with the curiosity of an explorer.

Networking: Build a network of like-minded individuals. Attend industry events, join online forums, and connect on professional platforms. Your tribe will keep you informed, inspired, and ready to tackle the latest technological challenges.

Integrating New Media into Your Strategy

- Data-Driven Decision Making: In a world flooded with information, data is your guiding light. Invest in analytics tools to understand your audience's behavior. Adapt your strategies based on real-time data, ensuring your advertising efforts are always on target.

- Agility in Campaigns: Rigidity is the enemy of progress. Stay nimble in your advertising campaigns. Monitor their performance, and be ready to pivot if something isn't working. Agility ensures you're always one step ahead of the competition.

During the process, expect roadblocks. Ads may not perform as expected, or a new platform may not yield the anticipated results. Fear not. Instead, consider these challenges as opportunities to refine and improve your strategies.

Ever felt overwhelmed by the sheer volume of tech updates? You're not alone. Embrace the overwhelm as a sign of growth. Ask yourself: How can I turn this challenge into an opportunity? How can I leverage these advancements to stand out in my field?

Tap into the wisdom of industry leaders and reputable sources to fortify your strategies. For the latest tech trends, turn to reliable sources such as Wired, TechCrunch, and Harvard Business Review.

Ensure your compass is calibrated. Review each step, refine your language, and eliminate any linguistic turbulence. A well-proofed guide is your best co-pilot.

As we conclude this exploration,remember adapting to changing technologies is not a one-time task; it's a dynamic process. Stay informed, be agile, and always be ready to ride the next wave of innovation. The tech world waits for no one, but armed with knowledge, you'll not only stay afloat but surf to success in the ever-changing sea of possibilities.

Future Legal Landscapes: Ethical Advertising in a Changing World

Staying ahead means more than just catchy slogans and eye-catching visuals. This chapter dives into the ethical and regulatory considerations that will shape the advertising landscape of the future. Having the key to not just surviving but thriving in this dynamic environment.

Buckle up, as we explore ethical advertising in a changing world and prepare you for the regulatory changes that lie ahead.

We'll break it down into bite-sized pieces, explaining the key aspects you need to grasp to navigate the advertising terrain confidently.

The Importance of Ethical Advertising: Ever wondered why ethical advertising matters? We'll explore how it builds trust, enhances brand reputation, and keeps you on the right side of the law. Think of it as the secret sauce for long-term success.

Preparing for Regulatory Changes: Regulations are like the weather – unpredictable. Learn how to anticipate and adapt to regulatory changes without breaking a sweat. We'll provide practical tips to future-proof your advertising strategy.

Building an Ethical Advertising Strategy: Ready to take the reins? We'll guide you through building an ethical advertising strategy that not only complies with regulations but also resonates with your audience. It's not just about playing by the rules; it's about winning hearts and minds.

According to industry experts and regulatory bodies, staying ethical in advertising is not just a choice – it's a necessity. We've gathered insights from trusted sources to ensure you're equipped with the latest and most reliable information.

In the fast-paced world of advertising, pitfalls are inevitable. We'll share practical advice based on real-world experiences to help you navigate the common challenges, ensuring your ethical advertising ship sails smoothly.

Ever felt overwhelmed by the advertising maze? We get it. Join us as we unravel the complexities together, addressing the concerns you might have and answering the questions you didn't even know you had.

Check out the links for more in-depth insights and studies that support our adventure through ethical advertising. We've done the digging so you can focus on conquering the advertising landscape.

Before we wrap up, a quick check for any loose ends. We want this guide to be as polished as your future advertising strategy. Let's make sure every word counts.

Now that we've covered the ins and outs of ethical advertising, you're not just equipped; you're empowered. As the advertising landscape evolves, so will you – confidently, ethically, and with a strategic edge.

Chapter 11
Building Lasting Customer Relationships Through Ads

In the digital jungle of modern advertising, creating an ad that not only catches the eye but also forms a lasting bond with the audience is like finding a four-leaf clover in a field of shamrocks. It's rare, special, and totally worth the hunt. This elusive goal is not just about selling a product; it's about building a relationship. Think of it as the difference between a fleeting Tinder date and a soulmate connection. Yes, we're getting deep here, but stay with me!

Let's break it down into digestible nuggets:

- Tell a Story, Don't Just Sell a Product: People love stories, not sales pitches. Craft your ads to tell a tale that resonates with your audience. Remember that time when you heard a story and thought, "That's so me!"? That's the golden ticket.

- Humor is Your Secret Weapon: A little laughter goes a long way. Ads that tickle the funny bone tend to stick in the memory longer. Just don't force it – nobody likes a try-hard comedian.

- Be Bold, Be Different: Challenge the norm. If everyone is zigging, it's time to zag. But don't just be different for the sake of it. Your uniqueness should have a purpose, like a peacock's plumage – stunning and functional.

- Actionable Advice, Not Just Fluff: Offer something of value. Tips, tricks, life hacks – anything that your audience can actually use. It's like giving a fishing rod, not just a fish.

- Leverage Expert Quotes: Include thoughts from industry leaders. It's like having a celebrity endorsement without the celebrity price tag.

- Use Metaphors and Analogies: They are the spices of the writing world. Just the right amount can enhance the flavor of your content.

- Back it Up With Data: As much as we love stories and humor, numbers don't lie. A statistic can sometimes hit harder than a well-crafted joke.

Now, let's get real with some examples. Remember the ad that made you cry? Or the one that made you laugh so hard you shared it with all your friends? Those ads had something in common: they made you *feel* something. They didn't just shout discounts at you; they whispered an experience into your ear.

Consider the impact of feedback loops in human interaction. Ads that invite a response, like a question or a challenge, can create a conversation. It's like tossing a ball to someone – they're more likely to toss it back.

Finally, let's talk about the elephant in the room – AI in advertising. Yes, AI can generate content, but it can't replicate human emotion (yet). That's where you, the creative genius, come in. Inject your personality, your experiences, and your unique perspective into your ads.

In conclusion, building lasting customer relationships through ads is about weaving a tapestry of stories, humor, boldness, and wisdom. It's about creating something that sticks in the heart, not just the mind. So, go ahead, be that rare four-leaf clover in the advertising field. Your audience is waiting for something real. And who knows, you might just find that in this quest to connect with your customers, you end up connecting with yourself too.

Building Bridges, Not Barriers: The Art of Ads in Relationship Building

In the vast landscape of marketing, one tool stands out as a bridge connecting brands and consumers - ads. The power of advertising goes beyond promoting products; it's about forging lasting connections, understanding customers, and fostering trust. Ads not as interruptions but as companions towards meaningful relationships. In this exploration of Subchapter 10.1, we uncover the pivotal role ads play in relationship building.

Understanding Customers: Ever felt lost in a sea of options? Your customers have too. Ads are your navigation guide, helping them navigate the waves of choices. Understand their customers, and your ad becomes the lighthouse they seek.

Ads as a Tool for Engagement: It's not just about grabbing attention; it's about keeping it. Dive into the art of engagement through ads. Be a storyteller, evoke emotions, and create an experience that lingers in the minds of your audience.

Creating Trust Through Advertising: Trust - the cornerstone of any relationship. Your ads should be more than flashy graphics. They should be a promise, a commitment. Learn the secrets of building trust through advertising, and you'll have a customer for life.

According to a study by Nielsen, 83% of consumers trust recommendations from people they know. Apply this wisdom to ads. Make your brand a friend, not a salesperson.

Solutions on Potential Pitfalls

- Understanding Customers: Map your customer's experience like an explorer. Identify pain points and let your ads be the solution. Neglecting the experience might lead to misplaced ads, causing confusion rather than clarity.

- Ads as a Tool for Engagement: Craft your ad like a compelling story. Make it relatable, and watch your audience become part of the narrative. Overloading with information can drown the story. Keep it concise to maintain engagement.

- Creating Trust Through Advertising: Consistency is key. Ensure your messaging aligns with your actions. Let your ads reflect the genuine character of your brand. Contradictions between ad promises and actual experiences erode trust faster than you can build it.

Have you ever bought something because the ad felt like a friend's recommendation? We've all been there. Let's unlock the secrets of creating ads that resonate, that build relationships rather than just sell products.

As we navigate through this process, ensure your message is crystal clear. Revisit each step, polish the edges, and let your words flow seamlessly. The magic is in the details.

In this voyage through the role of ads in relationship building, we've explored the intricacies of understanding customer experience, engagement, and trust. As you embark on your own advertising expedition, remember, it's not just about selling; it's about building connections. Ads, when wielded with insight and empathy, become the catalysts for relationships that stand the test of time.

So, as you dive into the world of ads, armed with the wisdom of understanding customer experiences and the art of engagement, don't just sell a product - sell an experience, a connection. Let your ads be the foundation of lasting relationships, where trust is the currency, and your brand is a companion on the adventure of life. Build bridges, not barriers, and watch your audience become not just customers but advocates, bound to your brand by the threads of shared experiences and mutual trust.

The Power of Personalization: Tailoring Ads to Your Unique Preferences

Ever wondered if advertising now syncs effortlessly with your tastes? In this era, understanding how to craft personalized ads isn't just beneficial—it's essential. If you're curious about how to engage your audience in a more meaningful way, you're in the right place. Let's dive into the world of personalized and customized advertising.

Understanding Personalized Messaging

- Why it Works: Personalized messaging resonates because it

speaks directly to the individual, making them feel understood and valued. It's not just about using their name; it's about understanding their needs, preferences, and behaviors.

- The Human Touch: Incorporate elements that reflect an understanding of the customer's lifestyle, interests, and past interactions. This creates a connection that goes beyond the transactional.

The Role of Data in Customization

- Data-Driven Insights: Leverage customer data ethically to tailor your messaging. Understand their browsing habits, purchase history, and even social media activity to create ads that feel personal.

- Balancing Privacy and Personalization: Always respect privacy boundaries. Use data transparently and with permission, ensuring that customers feel secure and respected.

Crafting Tailored Ads

- Segmentation is Key: Break down your audience into smaller segments based on common characteristics or behaviors. This allows for more targeted messaging.

- Dynamic Content: Use dynamic content in your ads that changes based on who is viewing it. This could mean different images, text, or offers, depending on the viewer's profile.

Personalization in Action

- Case Studies: Look at successful personalized ad campaigns. What did they do right? How did they speak to their audience's needs and preferences?

- Feedback Loop: Implement a system to gather feedback on your ads. This helps in refining and improving your approach to personalization.

Overcoming Challenges in Personalization

- Avoiding the 'Creepy' Factor: Be cautious not to overstep. There's a fine line between personalized and invasive. Strive for relevance without intrusion.

- Technological Limitations: Sometimes the technology isn't there yet to fully realize your vision. Work within these constraints creatively and innovatively.

In wrapping up, remember that the essence of personalized advertising is about creating a connection. It's a blend of art and science, requiring an understanding of data, technology, and human psychology. Personalization isn't just a marketing strategy; it's a commitment to understanding and valuing your audience as individuals. By respecting their preferences and privacy, and by providing them with relevant and engaging content, you're not just selling a product or service; you're building a relationship.

In this rapidly evolving digital landscape, those who master the art of personalization will not only see increased engagement and conversions but will also build lasting relationships with their customers. It's not just about the data or the technology; it's about the human connection. And that, my friends, is the real power of personalized advertising.

Crafting Connections: Customer Engagement and Retention in Advertising

Consumers are bombarded with countless ads every day, standing out is not just about being seen—it's about being remembered and valued. This is your guide to transforming advertising into an art form that not only captures attention but nurtures lasting relationships with your customers.

The Essence of Customer Engagement

- Building a Connection: Engagement is about creating a meaningful relationship between your brand and your audience. It's not just about grabbing attention; it's about holding it and making it count.

- Engagement Strategies: Use storytelling in your ads to evoke emotions. Host interactive campaigns on social media, encouraging user participation and feedback.

Loyalty Through Advertising

- Beyond the First Purchase: Loyalty isn't won overnight. It's cultivated through consistent, positive experiences with your brand.

- Rewarding Loyalty: Implement loyalty programs advertised through your campaigns. Offer exclusive deals or early access to loyal customers, making them feel valued and special.

Retention Techniques in the Advertising Realm

- Understanding Retention: It's far more cost-effective to retain an existing customer than to acquire a new one. Retention is about keeping your customers interested and invested in your brand.

- Retention-Focused Campaigns: Create ads that showcase customer success stories or how your product/service has evolved based on customer feedback. This shows that you listen and adapt, fostering trust and loyalty.

Measuring Engagement and Loyalty

- Metrics Matter: Track engagement metrics like click-through rates, time spent on ads, and social media interactions. For loyalty, monitor repeat purchase rates and referrals.

- Continuous Improvement: Use these metrics to refine your strategies. Understand what resonates with your audience and what doesn't, and adjust accordingly.

Navigating Challenges in Customer Engagement and Retention

- Overcoming Ad Fatigue: In a world cluttered with ads, how do you stand out? Be creative, be different, but most importantly, be authentic. Authenticity resonates with the audience.

- Maintaining Consistency: Consistency in your message, brand voice, and quality is key. Inconsistency can lead to a loss of trust and interest.

In conclusion, remember that at the heart of successful advertising is a deep understanding of and respect for the customer. It's not just about selling a product; it's about creating an experience, a connection that goes beyond a mere transaction. By focusing on engagement and retention, you're investing in a relationship that will not only increase the lifetime value of your customers but also turn them into advocates for your brand.

Your experience in advertising should always be evolving, adapting to new trends, technologies, and, most importantly, the changing needs of your customers. In this ever-changing landscape, those who listen, understand, and act on their customers' needs will not just survive but thrive. Your ads are more than just a way to sell; they are a way to connect, engage, and build a community around your brand. Keep this in mind, and you'll not only capture the market but also capture hearts.

Chapter 12
Conclusion

N avigating the dynamic world of advertising space is like steering a ship through ever-changing seas. The adventure you had with "Ad Space Profits" is not just about understanding the vast ocean of advertising opportunities but mastering the art of sailing through them effectively. From the foundational principles of ad space to the innovative approaches in digital and outdoor advertising, this book has equipped you with the tools and knowledge to not just float but to soar.

In the world of modern marketing, ad space emerges as a vibrant thread, connecting businesses with their audiences in a dance of supply and demand. As you've discovered, mastering the basics of ad space is critical. It's about more than just selecting the right spot; it's about understanding the audience, designing ads that resonate, and measuring their impact. This understanding is your compass, guiding you through the complex world of advertising.

Digital ad space, with its myriad of possibilities, presents a landscape ripe for exploration. The strategies you've learned—SEO optimization, analytics-driven placement, and crafting click-worthy content—are your map and tools, helping you navigate the digital terrain. Remember, it's not just about being seen; it's about being seen by the right eyes.

Print advertising, often perceived as a relic of a bygone era, holds its own unique power. It's about tapping into the enduring value of tangibility. The lessons on crafting compelling print ads, choosing the right medium, and understanding the demographics are your anchor, ensuring your message holds weight and relevance.

Social media is a whirlwind of potential, a platform where creativity meets technology. Your newfound skills in creating engaging ads, using precision targeting, and leveraging the power of retargeting are your sails, catching the winds of trends and user behavior to propel your brand forward.

Outdoor advertising is where creativity meets the real world. Designing memorable outdoor ads and choosing strategic locations is not just an art; it's a science. This chapter has been your telescope, helping you see the opportunities that lie in the vast expanse of the physical world.

The niche ad spaces chapter opened your eyes to the beauty of specificity. Customizing ads for niche audiences and collaborating with influencers are like finding hidden treasures in the vast sea of advertising. These strategies are your divers, plunging deep into the waters to bring up pearls of targeted impact.

Ad copywriting is the soul of your campaign. The principles of persuasive copywriting, understanding your audience, and crafting calls to action are your quill and ink, writing the story of your brand in a way that resonates and compels.

Maximizing ROI in ad space investment is about turning your ads into assets. Understanding ROI components, optimizing ad spend, and leveraging ad tech are the gears of your engine, driving efficiency and effectiveness in your advertising endeavors.

As you prepare for the future of advertising, remember that it's a landscape constantly reshaped by technology and trends. Staying current with advancements, adapting to changing technologies, and navigating ethical considerations are your guiding stars, keeping you on course in an ever-evolving world.

Building lasting customer relationships through ads is about forging connections that go beyond transactions. Personalization, engagement strategies, and retention techniques are the bonds that tie your brand to your audience, turning fleeting encounters into enduring relationships.

As this book comes to a close, remember that the world of ad space is a canvas, and you are the artist. With the tools, knowledge, and strategies you've gained, you're now equipped to paint a masterpiece of successful advertising. Go forth and make your mark, knowing that in the realm of ad space, the only limit is your creativity.